Warfare: Stop Attracting It!

By

Jeremy Lopez

Warfare: Stop Attracting It!

By Dr. Jeremy Lopez

Copyright © 2019

Published by Identity Network

P.O. Box 383213 Birmingham, AL 35238

www.IdentityNetwork.net

ENDORSEMENT

"You are put on this earth with incredible potential and a divine destiny. This powerful, practical man shows you how to tap into powers you didn't even know you had." – Brian Tracy – Author, The Power of Self Confidence

"I found myself savoring the concepts of the Law of Attraction merging with the Law of Creativity until slowly the beautiful truths seeped deeper into my thirsty soul. I am called to be a Creator! My friend, Dr. Jeremy Lopez, has a way of reminding us of our eternal 'I-Am-ness' while putting the tools in our hands to unlock our endless creative potential with the Divine mind. As a musical composer, I'm excited to explore, with greater understanding, the infinite realm of possibilities as I place fingers on my piano and whisper, 'Let there

be!'" – Dony McGuire, Grammy Award winning artist and musical composer

"Jeremy dives deep into the power of consciousness and shows us that we can create a world where the champion within us can shine and how we can manifest our desires to live a life of fulfillment. A must read!" – Greg S. Reid – Forbes and Inc. top rated Keynote Speaker

"I have been privileged to know Jeremy Lopez for many years, as well as sharing the platform with him at a number of conferences. Through this time, I have found him as a man of integrity, commitment, wisdom, and one of the most networked people I have met. Jeremy is an entrepreneur and a leader of leaders. He has amazing insights into leadership competencies and values. He has a passion to ignite this latent potential within individuals and organizations and provide ongoing development

and coaching to bring about competitive advantage and success. I would recommend him as a speaker, coach, mentor, and consultant." – Chris Gaborit – Learning Leader, Training & Outsourcing Expert, Entrepreneur

CONTENTS

Preface
Introduction
War in the Heavens
The War is Over
Images and Idols
Life and Death
Awakenings
Transference
Resist and Repent
The Goodness
Outer Darkness
Forgetting the Monsters
The Art of War
About the Author
Additional Works

PREFACE

What is it about the dark that causes us to fear? Is it the sense of the unknown and the unfamiliarity that comes when we feel we cannot see? Or is it, even more so, a deeply ingrained inner drive, innate within humanity, which seems to beckon us to fight against anything and everything we do not understand? From the dawn of even the earliest civilizations, the apparent war between the light and the dark – between those things we call "good" and those things we call "evil" – has given rise to a never ending and ceaseless belief in the need for warfare. Throughout decades of prophetic ministry, I have witnessed, firsthand, the effects of a belief in spiritual warfare. I have witnessed what could only be described as "miraculous," and the supernatural has become natural to me in my own journey of faith in ministry. I have witnessed lives transformed through the awakening power of the Holy Spirit. I have seen moments of turnabout so very distinct and so very undeniable that they left no doubt the existence of spiritual realities. And I have also seen, firsthand, moments that seemed to be so very dark.

The 1980's saw the rise of spiritual warfare. Throughout circles of faith, particularly within the more Pentecostal and charismatic camps within the Christian faith – particularly within the prophetic renewal – various teachings began to emerge regarding the concept of spiritual warfare. From new teachings regarding "intercession" to strange teachings regarding "demons" and "demonology," many prophetic voices of the time began to rise to prominence, touting a very frightening message: "We are under attack." For decades, it seemed, much more was being said about demons, Satan, the devil and his wiles, than was ever mentioned about the power of the Spirit. They seemed to be very dark days, indeed. However, the teachings were nothing new. Although the concept of spiritual warfare seemed to find an entirely new audience in that generation and find its footing, the premise of spiritual warfare is one as old as humanity itself. To this day, though, the ramifications of such teachings and such ideas still permeate the landscape of faith, as day by day sincere men and women continue to believe that life within the Kingdom equates to a life of constant struggle – a life of constant attack.

My dear, friend, I feel the need to write these words to you, and I say with no exaggeration that this book has been, quite literally, more than twenty years in the making. Throughout my years in ministry, I have been so very blessed and so privileged to have connected with audiences across the globe. Through the outreach of Identity Network, I have been so honored to have shared the stages of conferences and services with many of the other notable pioneers of the prophetic movement and other generals of the faith. I witnessed, firsthand, as individuals by the thousands came forward to share testimony after testimony of how they continued to be attacked, suffering debilitating bouts of oppression – some even going as far as to call it "possession." In those days, I was even in attendance in services that seemed to rival even the most terrifying of horror films, as those claiming to be under the influence of dark and malevolent forces began to manifest their apparent dual natures for all to see. But then, just as quickly as it had all began, it ceased just as quickly. Often, in a moment – in the twinkling of an eye – the sense of peace would envelop the participants, overshadowing who had only moments before been the apparent "victims" of demonic attack.

More than twenty years ago, all of this changed for me in an instant – quite literally in the twinkling of an eye. As clearly as I have ever heard the voice of the inner Kingdom of Heaven within me, I heard these words: "The church will have what it preaches." In that moment, I found myself changed. What would happen, I thought, if we simply stopped promoting fear-based religious paranoia and hyperbole? What would we begin to encounter if, rather than focusing on the elements of spiritual warfare, we began, rather, to focus upon the abundant life? Deliverance services, as theatrical and as camp as they are, make for very interesting and entertaining television ministries. They draw enormous crowds. They bring abundance in finance to the local church. But are they Biblical? My friend, even now, there are many sincere men and women of faith who would wish you to believe that Jesus, throughout his earthly life and ministry, spoke just as much concerning "Satan" and "demons" as he did about the glory of spiritual awakening. Contrary to what you have been led to believe about life in the Kingdom, though, this is simply not true. Spiritual warfare is one of the greatest and most damnable lies propagated by fear-based religion, and, as you will soon see, it has no part within a truly victorious life.

Now, within this generation, I feel led through the unction of the Holy Spirit to completely dismantle and to completely destroy, once and for all, the erroneous, unfounded, shallow, unbiblical, often comical, and often completely illogical teachings regarding spiritual warfare. As a testament to the power of the inner Kingdom of Heaven and as a testimony of a truly overcoming and victorious life, I now offer this teaching and this revelation for the first time ever. It is time that you become free. It is time you cease from fearing. Above all else, though, it is time you stop fighting needless and pointless wars. As you will soon see, right now within your very own life, not only are you experiencing exactly what you have been led to proclaim, but you now have *exactly* what you believe. As you will soon discover, the war ended a long, long time ago.

INTRODUCTION

The constant struggle between the light and the dark is ubiquitous throughout all human history as even from the earliest civilizations mankind has grappled with its understanding of "good" and "evil." From the very beginning of man's religious zeal, organized religion has always sought to capitalize upon humanity's most basic, primal fear – the fear of the "dark." From even the earliest civilizations upon the earth, primitive cultures have long-since equated darkness with the malevolent and the demonic. From an anthropological perspective, every evening, as the sun went down, many primitive civilizations viewed the looming darkness as a sign that the "underworld" was being given free reign and rule until the next morning. Many feared even going outdoors again until the sun rose the following morning. From the apparent contradictions of "light" and "dark," myths were created and folklore began to abound. Then came the anthropomorphic projectionism which always accompanies humanity's fear of the unknown. In an attempt to rationalize the unknown, the mind begins to create its own stories – triggering its own visualization. In an instant, then, the fear begins to become all the more real, as it's given a face, human characteristics, and personality, taking on a life of its own.

Organized religion has played upon this fear of the dark more than any other force in human history, creating dogma to define the world of darkness, yielding credence to and providing a platform to the rulers of darkness, and even going as far to craft the erroneous narrative which suggests, "the stronger the faith, the greater the attack of the enemy." As absurd as it may sound to the natural, logical mind, I know that if you have spent any time delving into popular teachings regarding spiritual warfare you relate completely to what I am sharing. But what role, if any, does spiritual warfare play within the life of an individual? For that matter, is it truly a Biblical concept? In order to better understand this question, we must begin to delve into the scriptures, and to grasp the concept of spiritual warfare, we must also begin to examine the power of belief. To better understand the enormous power of belief, though, we must also begin to examine the creative power of thought and visualization. After all, it was Jesus, himself, who so transcendentally taught that we will have *exactly* what we believe in.

On December 26th, 1973, a film was released to the world which changed not only the history of cinema but also impacted the way in which much of the world viewed spirituality and faith. The film was *The Exorcist*. Based upon the novel and the subsequent screenplay by William

Peter Blatty, the writing and the film depicted the concept of demonic possession as never before. So visceral was the depiction, in fact, that churches across the nation protested and boycotted the film. Some of the most notable and prestigious evangelists of the faith, in fact, gave press releases calling the film itself "dangerous." Though I must admit I'm not a fan of horror films and would much rather spend my quality, leisure time reading a good book, I must admit that even I found myself questioning why such uproar had been caused. What could possibly put the church in such a state of panic and shock? And for what reason? Was it because the church truly believes in the dark and malevolent elements of the spiritual world as it claims, or was it something else? Was it something even more sinister? Could it be, rather, that organized religion simply wanted to control the monopoly on teachings regarding demons and demonology? Could it be that religion, as a means to control, simply wanted to control the narrative regarding spiritual warfare? What is it, really, that causes the church to live in such overwhelming fear? I could not help but question.

Shortly after the turn of the millennium, in the height of what some might refer to as the prophetic and charismatic renewal, I was asked to be guest minister at a prophetic conference in Anaheim. I was honored to be included upon the roster alongside many of the notable teachers and pioneers of the prophetic and the apostolic. Having become familiar with my own prophetic gifting and having begun to write books of my own, doors were opened for me that placed me upon a world stage. The final night of the three night conference had been billed as a "deliverance" service. There were thousands in attendance. I watched as countless individuals came forward, after being called upon by various, local ministers from within the community. The scene was one of pandemonium and bedlam, as those suffering from supposed "possession" were given prayer. It was loud. It was very loud. In the midst of the pandemonium, a young woman was brought upon the stage to me by a few of the local ministers from the neighboring city. I will never forget the sight – or the sound. Her hair was disheveled. There were tears in her eyes. She was groaning and hissing – snarling and screaming loudly as prayers for her were offered by the other ministers. But with every prayer, she groaned even more loudly and became even more defiant and unruly.

"Jeremy, we need you to pray with us," one of the ministers said. "We need you to agree with us for her deliverance." And then, in an instant, under the unction of the Holy Spirit came a sense of radical discernment which shook me to my core. This dear woman did not have a "demonic" issue. She had a belief issue.

And the surrounding crowd seemed all too happy to play into it and to capitalize upon it. I looked at her, and I pulled her toward me. I said to her in a loving but firm voice, quite simply, "I refuse to play into this religious nonsense with you! Be quiet! Go back to your seat. And never ever do this again!" Just as quickly as her supposed "manifestation" had begun, it ended just as quickly. To the shock and to the amazement of some and to the bewilderment of the other ministers, she immediately stopped. She became silent. She wiped her face. And she returned to her seat. She's now a successful business owner, and I was informed that after that night she was never again oppressed or attacked by the "enemy." I share this very real illustration with you, my friend, to say, quite simply, that everything stems from belief. If you now find yourself living a life of constant struggle, under constant attack and seeming to continually face the onslaught of "Hell" in your life, the reason, quite simply, is because of what you believe. I promise you that the moment you begin to change your beliefs, you will begin to change your life.

Beliefs are real, insomuch as each thought is infused with the creative power of the Godhead. Every thought dwelt upon will in some way manifest and be brought into the physical world. If you believe in warfare, you will live a life consumed with spiritual warfare and attack. If you believe yourself to be a Creator within the realm of the inner Kingdom of Heaven, though, the fear will end just as quickly as it began. Today, within Christendom, there are countless teachers, ministers, and so-called prophets who would have you believe that within life in the Kingdom, encounters of attack are just a necessary evil which must be tolerated. Many of these so-called leaders would even have you to believe that in order to have faith requires having to continually face a barrage of attack after attack doing spiritual warfare. You're all too familiar with it, I'm sure. We were told to "bind" this and to "rebuke" that. We were told to "Plead the Blood" over this and that. If it didn't feel good, we were told to simply "stand against it" and "cast it out" invoking the name of the LORD. I often joke that the Dark Ages never truly ended. Today, within religion, there is just as much paranoia, fear, and primitive ideology as ever before. And believe me when I say to you that religion wants to keep it that way! Why? Because it's good for business.

Is it Biblical though? That is to say, throughout the entirety of the scriptures, with each account of deliverance and each account of supposed demonic attack, what role did the concept of spiritual warfare truly play? As you will soon begin to see, as we delve into the greater truths of the inner Kingdom of Heaven, contrary to what you have been led to believe, throughout his earthly life and ministry, Jesus never once struggled with spiritual warfare. He never felt the need to. Contrary to what is now commonly taught within the Pentecostal and charismatic circles of Christianity, there was never a struggle as we were once led to believe. There was never a fight. In fact, as you will soon realize, there was never once even a real confrontation. Rather, there was simply a knowing – a knowing so real and so transcendent, in fact, that with a simple expression of thought and with one utterance, atmospheres changed. Because the beliefs of others were changed. Religion, strangely enough, though it preaches and proclaims the sovereignty of the LORD, always seems to contradict itself by simultaneously painting Jesus as this weak and anemic, emaciated person who always seems to be fighting against the devil. Have you noticed this? Oddly enough, the same religion which boldly proclaims to the world that Christ is LORD of all seems to be the exact same religion that simultaneously teaches life in the Kingdom is one in which believers must constantly do spiritual warfare on a daily basis. And so I would ask, why the apparent contradiction? Logically speaking, which one is the true reality of the matter? Is He, in fact, LORD of all, or is there something else – some darkness – existing beyond His realm of reach and his scope of control?

My dear friend, I sense that you are now reading these words because you are now facing the onslaught of attack which accompanies spiritual warfare. I sense you being paralyzed by crippling and debilitating fear. Perhaps, as you read these words, it's been weeks since you've actually enjoyed a full, restful night's sleep. The nightmares have plagued you. Panic and paranoia have kept you awake for days on end, as you have been taught that the enemy, like a roaring lion, is determined to destroy your life, your career, your family, and your finances. But I would respectfully and humbly ask, what would happen if you could realize that simply isn't the case and that it never truly has been? What if you could begin to see, through the scriptures, that the enemy has been your very own beliefs all along and that the battlefield, truly, has been within your very own mind? Most importantly, though, what if you could begin to change your beliefs? What if you could determine in your heart and within your mind, today, that you will finally, once and for all, abandon and completely dismantle unbiblical thinking? For far, far too long, you've held to religious fear because you have erroneously been led to believe that you have no choice in the matter. And so, as a result, you've said, "Well, this is just the way it has to be." My friend, nothing could be any more of a religious lie.

By now, perhaps, you may now find yourself assuming that I in no way believe in an enemy at all. Nothing could be any further from the truth. Just as Jesus said throughout his own earthly life and ministry, there absolutely *is*, in fact, a very real enemy and, furthermore, there *is* a very real and very literal war being waged. The true war being waged, though, is not what you have been taught to believe. In fact, this war, rather than being fueled in the literal heavens, is being waged in the true realm of Heaven – the inner realm within your very own self. As you will soon see, as we begin to examine even more closely the great truth regarding spiritual warfare, not only will you begin to realize that the battles you face are self-created; you will, for the first time ever, finally be able to recognize yourself as a victorious Creator within your own life. To build a new paradigm, though, requires first dismantling unbiblical beliefs and making the conscious choice to once and for all put away childish things. My friend, it is time to grow within the Kingdom.

For decades, through the evangelistic and prophetic work of Identity Network, I have been so very privileged and humbled to have seen, firsthand, countless individuals just like you begin to access the realm of greater abundance. Something truly remarkable begins to happen, in fact, the moment an individual, through the leading of the Spirit, becomes awakened to the greater truths of the inner Kingdom which Jesus spoke of and continually taught. Something, well, very supernatural begins to transpire the instant the mind becomes awakened to the truth that a life of constant struggle, constant fighting, and constant attack is not only unnecessary but is actually quite the antithesis of the abundant life. Today, as you now find yourself reading these words, I wish to make you a very real promise as you continue onward. This promise is a covenantal promise of agreement – a bond of partnership. If you will remain open to the leading voice of the Holy Spirit and will enter into this journey with an openness and a willingness to once and for all tear down and dismantle the unbiblical concepts you have for far too long idolized within your own life, I promise you that freedom will come. And when freedom comes, never again will you ever be the same.

A life lived to face the constant barrage of attack is a life lived in lack and uncertainty. Show me a life lived constantly engaging in spiritual warfare and I will show you a life being lived beneath its means. It's all too common, really. "The devil is attacking my finances." "I rebuke the spirit of lack and poverty." You've, I'm sure, heard it all before. And where relationships are concerned, well, spiritual warfare, even there, is continuously waged. "I bind my husband's negativity in the name of Jesus." "I rebuke my wife's controlling spirit." As, perhaps, outlandish as such statements might seem, they serve to reflect the erroneous lie which rests at the heart of all spiritual warfare. And why is this so? The answer is because all spiritual warfare entices the warrior to continue to look outward rather than inward – projecting onto others the issues of the heart. Jesus made it plain throughout his earthly ministry that belief is the most powerful force in all existence. Through his many notable parables and miraculous healings and, yes, even in his dealings with the elements of darkness, he revealed to humanity the power of the inner Kingdom, reminding us all that we possess the power to have whatsoever we truly believe. And so now I would ask you, my fellow seeker, what do you truly believe in?

As I found myself, all those years ago, questioning the true cause of fear, inspired by the Holy Spirit to analyze the true meaning of spiritual warfare, I began to find myself even more inspired than ever before to share the truth of victory with the world. Something begins to happen, you see, the moment that one begins to become awakened to the truth of the inner Kingdom. All of the fear begins to simply vanish away. And, then, when fear leaves, the impossible suddenly becomes possible. There is a reason the scriptures make it plain that perfect love casts out all fear. The moment you begin to become awakened to the truth of the love of GOD within your life, all of the constant attacks begin to vanish, melting away underneath the weight of the glory of heavenly, Kingdom truth. As the scriptures declare, you shall know the truth and the truth shall make you free. Truth, in and of itself, though, has never made anyone free. It is only the truth that can be realized – the truth that is *known* – which brings about change. As we delve into the truths of the inner Kingdom of Heaven and examine the spiritual,

Biblical truth regarding spiritual warfare, we will not only dismantle the unbiblical, unscriptural illusions that religion has created, but we will also dismantle even the ability to fear. Can you imagine not even being able to fear? Imagine such a life. You would never be the same again.

WAR IN THE HEAVENS

"And there was war in Heaven…"

In order to begin to see the greater, more transcendent truths regarding the spiritual realities of the Kingdom of Heaven which Jesus spoke of, one must first understand that the scriptures and the truths have always been much more sacred and much more spiritual than religious traditions have ever dared admit. As a lifelong student of the sacred text of the scriptures, what I have long-since found is that when examining the writings – particularly the more Apocalyptic writings of the Apostle John – it is essential to bear in mind that the writings were transcribed because of a vision. The Apostle John, himself, having been exiled on the Isle of Patmos for proclaiming the message of the Kingdom, makes it clear in his own words that he was "in the Spirit" while he was shown the vision that would serve as the basis of the Book of Revelation. *"I was in the Spirit on the Lord's day." (Revelation 1:10 KJV)* Historically and theologically speaking, in order to better understand the context of the Apocalyptic writings of John, one must also consider the circumstances surrounding his exile to the Isle of Patmos. The newly established "church," then, was still in a very infantile stage of its existence, having been birthed at Pentecost only decades before. When the holy city of Jerusalem fell to the Roman Empire in 70 A.D., a time of even greater persecution came upon the church. Many were martyred for the cause of Christ. Others were exiled or imprisoned.

Having been heavily involved in prophetic ministry for decades, I can tell you that the Book of Revelation has been used more than all other books as the basis for end-time teachings.

Within the publishing arena, countless thousands of teachings exist from well-known Christian authors and prophetic teachers who use the Book of Revelation as a basis for discerning current, world events. The study of end-time events, or "eschatology," is not only the basis for many popular teachings within the Christian faith, but it is also one which brings with it perhaps the single, greatest element of fear. To better contextualize this overwhelming sense of fear and paranoia, one would simply need to look back to the turn of the millennium, to the great hoax of "Y2K." I still find it rather disheartening that to this very day not one single end-time prophetic scholar or televangelist has apologized for helping stoke the fire of fear within the church. It's as if it never happened – as if we were supposed to simply move on. Is it any wonder such end-time teachings within Christianity become the laughing stock of the world? My friend, the prophetic has absolutely nothing to do with times of apocalypse or, for that matter, even predictions of doom. Rather, the prophetic has everything to do with understanding the greater, seemingly more hidden truths.

The Book of Revelation, at the time of its writing, was never meant for the entire world; it was meant for a newly-formed, fledgling church which was still struggling to find its footing in the world. John, himself, even says as much in his writing by stating that the voice of the LORD had a very specific audience in mind. *"What thou seest, write in a book, and send it unto the seven churches which are in Asia; unto Ephesus, and unto Smyrna, and unto Pergamos, and unto Thyatira, and unto Sardis, and unto Philadelphia, and unto Laodicea."* *(Revelation 1:11 KJV)* Notice, if you will, the entire vision was given for a very specific purpose, at a very specific time, for a very specific target audience. I often like to say that the Revelation was a message to the early church which reminded it, "Even in this time of persecution, we will overcome." I share this, also, to say that if your concept of spiritual warfare is in any way based upon images of dragons, malevolent forces, continued attacks, and a literal "war" taking place in the spiritual dimension around you, I assure you that you are missing the point entirely. And yet, there *is* war raging in Heaven, even now in these more modern times. The fact that spiritual war is even such an issue within the church is proof positive that there is a very real dichotomy which seems to be in existence. To understand this "war," though, one must finally reassess the location of the battleground. Where is Heaven?

And there was war in heaven: Michael and his angels fought against the dragon; and the dragon fought and his angels, And prevailed not; neither was their place found any more in heaven. And the great dragon was cast out, that old serpent, called the Devil, and Satan, which deceiveth the whole world: he was cast out into the earth, and his angels were cast out with him. And I heard a loud voice saying in heaven, Now is come salvation, and strength, and the kingdom of our God, and the power of his Christ: for the accuser of our brethren is cast down, which accused them before our God day and night. And they overcame him by the blood of the Lamb, and by the word of their testimony; and they loved not their lives unto the death. Therefore rejoice, ye heavens, and ye that dwell in them. Woe to the inhabiters of the earth and of the sea! for the devil is come down unto you, having great wrath, because he knoweth that he hath but a short time. (Revelation 12:7-12 KJV) Even in the midst of turmoil, at a time of great persecution for the early church, the vision served as a reminder that overcoming belief and strong faith would yield the victory.

And so, to us, now in this modern time, what could be gleaned by such a vision? What are we, today, to learn from this where the element of spiritual warfare is concerned? To answer this, I feel compelled to say that if you now find yourself daily plagued by crippling and debilitating, paralyzing fear and paranoia, always feeling led to rebuke and to cast down and to constantly fight and to war against, you are keeping alive a very real war within yourself. Heaven, as Jesus emphatically stated throughout his earthly life and ministry, has never been some distant or far-off place, reserved solely for some distant, future time. Heaven, rather, is the realm within every person. Heaven is the *inner* world – not some *outer* world. *"And when he was demanded of the Pharisees, when the kingdom of God should come, he answered them and said, The kingdom of God cometh not with observation: Neither shall they say, Lo here! or, lo there! for, behold, the kingdom of God is within you." (Luke 17:20-21 KJV)* In his own words, Jesus makes the bold and emphatically transcendent declaration that the realm and the rule of Heaven is *within*. Knowing this, then, we are beginning to be given a glimpse of the battlefield where all spiritual warfare takes place. It takes place within our very own selves.

Throughout years of prophetic ministry, what I have found and what I continue to see is that the wars we fight are always, always wars which are self-created and self-imposed. There is never any exception to this, as you will soon discover and begin to realize as we delve even further into the scriptures. By now you must find yourself already beginning to reevaluate and to reassess the meaning of spiritual warfare. However, let us for a moment, just as a way to appease the religious minds of the world, now ask a very hypothetical question. "What if the war *is* literal?" Ponder that for a moment. Let's say, purely for the sake of hypothetical conjecture that the war in Heaven is, in fact, literally taking place now and is continually ongoing. Let us assume, hypothetically, that even now as you read these words that in this very moment, all around us in some spiritual dimension, there are angels battling demons, demons seeking to attack humans, demons attempting to ruin your marriage and your business and your finances, and ongoing battles being sparked all around us at all times. Imagine that. For a moment, just picture that within your mind's eye. Let's also assume that, even right now, every believer is expected to take up arms and join in the fight.

And now, with that picture of warfare in mind, let us also assume that even now Heaven is a literal city existing in some distant, far-away place – a place where all believers will one day be caught up to. Assume that in the paradise of this place, a place where we say the rule and reign of GOD is absolute and supreme, that even in the portals of heaven there are, even now, dark and malevolent forces now seeking to enter the throne room and overthrow the LORD Himself. Imagine, now, that in this supposed, apparent spiritual warfare, even now, the armies of Heaven actually have to resist in order to be victorious. My friend, as outlandish and as ludicrous as such imagery may seem to the natural mind, these images are the images of spiritual warfare. And now, lastly, purely as hypothetical conjecture, assume that this spiritual warfare in the heavens is continuing to take place, continuously ongoing, until some other future time. After all, is that not the basis of all religious teaching regarding spiritual warfare? If you view Heaven in this way and, furthermore, if you view the reality of Christ and the domain of the Kingdom in this way, then you are inadvertently also nullifying the entirety of the scriptures.

"For this purpose the Son of God was manifested, that he might destroy the works of the devil." (1 John 3:8 KJV) There is no grey area when considering the reality of the inner Kingdom of Heaven, my friend. Contrary to popular charismatic teachings regarding spiritual warfare and demonology and even the eschatological study of supposed end-time events, it is not only highly illogical but it is absolutely, downright impossible to view Jesus as victorious while also continuing to believe in spiritual warfare. A victorious Jesus and spiritual warfare simply cannot coexist! The two cannot be reconciled together! Either Jesus did, in fact, destroy the works of the devil or he didn't. Either the mission of the cross was a success or it was not a success. And to continue to hold to unbiblical beliefs regarding spiritual warfare is to simply say that Jesus failed in his attempt. You see, my dear friend, though for decades popular religious teachings have tried to

convince us that you and I, by our very nature, are at war with forces of darkness, such teachings are not only contradictory to the premise of the faith we hold to but are also the epitome of religious hypocrisy! Either He is LORD of all, or He is not. Either the rule and rein of the Kingdom is absolute and supreme or it is not. And if it is not, then, with all respect, what's the point of even believing in it?

I feel chains being broken around you even now, as you read these words. And if these words are offensive to you, then I'm thankful. My friend, for far, far too long, we've lived beneath our means, living lives of constant struggle and lack, always facing the onslaught of attack simply because we've been conditioned to believe in religious nonsense. Even children of a certain age cease to believe in monsters hiding underneath their beds. And then, when fear of the monsters does come, they simply turn on the lights and the darkness vanishes. It is high time we put away childish things regarding spiritual warfare once and for all. My friend, it is time we begin to grow in faith and move into a place of greater maturity and understanding. It's time to finally turn the lights on! It's time to see that the darkness is simply a lack of knowledge! When the Holy Spirit first began to inspire me with this revelation all those years ago, I felt the fear begin to leave. It was so freeing and so liberating. Who had I been warring against for so long? Who had I been seeking to rebuke and cast out and stand against for all those years? When the inspiration and the revelation of the Holy Spirit illuminated my mind all those years ago, I began to see, finally, that the wars we face are the wars within our very own selves, based upon our unbiblical beliefs.

If there truly *is* war being waged in Heaven, then that war is the inner war within our own selves, since Jesus emphatically declared that the Kingdom of Heaven is *within* us. And if the wars we wage are truly our own inner wars, how then do we cease from waging war? The answer might very well surprise you, my friend. And *that* is the purpose of my writing to you. What if I were to tell you that the spiritual warfare you face each and every day – the constant struggle and the constant, never ending battles – are the result of your very own beliefs? And that you face this spiritual warfare only because you've been conditioned to believe that you're supposed to? As difficult as it might seem for the religious mind to process, I assure you that is absolutely the truth of the matter. Remember, you will have *exactly* what you believe. And so, if you believe in the need for spiritual warfare then you will have spiritual warfare. If you believe that it's your mission to daily wage war in the heavens then you will have even more war. And if you believe that Jesus was not truly victorious, as the scriptures claim, then you will continue to fight. Furthermore, though, and perhaps even more importantly, if you do not believe that you, yourself, are victorious, then you will continue in your constant struggles. I stopped struggling a long, long time ago. I do not say that in a prideful way or to be boastful; I say that to simply say that I refuse to live a life of constant struggle because I simply don't believe in it. I choose to believe in an abundant and victorious life. I *choose* to believe in a universe that works for me and not against me.

There is absolutely nothing in existence more powerful than belief. What you choose to believe, you will ultimately attract. And what you attract will further serve to reinforce your belief. This is why change can often seem so very difficult to the natural, religious mind, with its constant feelings of depravity. "This is what I'm supposed to believe," it continuously says. It never becomes open to new ideas and to new revelations. Instead, it becomes content to settle for comfort of normality, comfortable to believe unbiblical truths, regardless of how uncomfortable and how draining they are. The religious mind – the mind opposed to the truth of the Creator – continuously says, "I have to fight." And, as a result, the war continues. Today, though, I feel inspired by the Holy Spirit to share with you a very simple truth – one which will not only change the course of your life if you will allow it but also one which will completely annihilate and eradicate all fear. This truth is very simple, yet transcendent, and, as you will soon discover, is the very basis of every parable, every miracle, every teaching, and, yes, even every encounter with the darkness within the earthly life and earthly ministry of Jesus. What is this truth, you might ask? The truth is this: "The war is over." Well, it's over, that is, if you can believe it to be.

THE WAR IS OVER

"You wage spiritual warfare only because you believe it's your job to do so." – Jeremy Lopez

It wasn't all that long ago, really, when the entire globe found itself enveloped in a literal war. Much like spiritual warfare, the ensuing results of this war were catastrophic. And the effects were deadly. In the midst of the Second World War, as the Allied and Axis powers collided, there was a sense of nationalism rarely seen, as each country engaged in conflict sought victory. Of the countries involved, though, few demonstrated the sense of nationalism quite like the Empire of Japan. Committed to defending the honor of the homeland while simultaneously advancing toward victory, Japanese militants devoted themselves to giving their final breaths to the cause of the Japanese motherland. This sense of nationalism was depicted even through the many pilots who flew in the skies. The use of "kamikaze" pilots made the Japanese force all the more deadly to engage with. *Kamikaze,* a Japanese term meaning "Divine wind," was a term used to refer to pilots who flew suicide missions during the war, using even their planes as weapons as a final act of defiance against their enemies. Bearing in mind this sense of nationalism, it isn't difficult to see the strong role the sense of honor and commitment play when considering the element of warfare. Literal warfare is much like spiritual warfare, in that regard, as belief and tradition fuel the ongoing fight.

There is no other story quite like that of Japanese militant Hiroo Onoda. In the mist of the conflict of the Second World War, Onoda was sent in 1944 to the island of Lubang, a small island in the western Philippines, to spy on American forces stationed there. The events that transpired were absolutely astounding. For Onoda, what began as a basic military exercise would come to define not only the remainder of his life but also the entire history of Japan's involvement in the war. Trained in guerilla warfare, Hiroo Onoda was tasked with gaining counter-intelligence at all cost, while hiding himself deep, deep within the heart of the island's jungles. When Allied forces defeated the Japanese Imperial army, Onoda continued his mission completely unaware of his country's surrender. He continued to evade capture. In fact, even when he received word that the war had ended, Onoda sincerely and firmly believed that those who made such claims were merely spies, determined to trick him into giving away his cover. Whenever he heard that Japan had surrendered and that the war was, indeed, over, he thought it could not possible be true. Astonishingly and miraculously, Hiroo Onoda remained in the jungles of Lubang, surviving on wild berries, continuing to gain his "counter-intelligence" for more than twenty-nine years *after* the war had come to a close – the entire time sincerely and firmly believing that he was had not yet been relieved of his imperial duties and that the war continued to wage on around him. Onoda was finally persuaded to come out of hiding in 1974, only *after* the man who had once been his commanding officer traveled to Lubang to inform Onoda that the war had, in fact, come to an end – nearly thirty years prior. While still wearing his battered old army uniform, Onoda emerged from the jungles, finally, and surrendered his sword.

Hiroo Onoda was later quoted as saying, "Every Japanese soldier was prepared for death, but as an intelligence officer I was ordered to conduct guerrilla warfare and not to die. I had to follow my orders as I was a soldier." When asked, years later, if he ever regretted the years seemingly spent wasted in the jungles of Lubang and questioned if he ever felt a sense of anger or sadness over the matter, he responded, simply, "I became an officer and I received an order. If I could not carry it out, I would feel shame. I am very competitive." When I first was made aware of the remarkable and somewhat tragic story of Hiroo Onoda, I found myself feeling a variety of mixed emotions. Imagine the dedication to the cause required for one to remain so faithful to a supposed mission. Onoda, by all accounts, did not remain in the jungle because of desire; he did so because of commitment to a cause he genuinely, wholeheartedly believed in. He continued to remain faithful to his orders, long, long after the war had ended. When viewed from the vantage point of a lesson in faithfulness, his story is one of inspiration. However, when viewed from the perspective of wasted years, the story seems almost overwhelmingly tragic and saddening.

When I began to ponder the message of this book regarding spiritual warfare, I realized that it would be impossible to share the revelation I had been given without also including the remarkable, almost unbelievable account of Onoda.

If ever there was a spiritual war being waged in any way, to any degree, it ended a long, long time ago. Yet, now, all this time later, as an act of your "faithfulness," you continue to fight, continuing to struggle, daily, living way beneath your means because you refuse to believe that the struggle is unnecessary. As a result of your beliefs, you continue to view every unexpected and apparent obstacle as merely an "attack" of the enemy. When hardship comes, it cannot possibly be that the universe is seeking to get your attention in an attempt to make you better, you believe. Instead, you think, it *must* be an attack of the enemy. When dealing with your difficult spouse, rather than realizing that perhaps you are much of the cause of the apparent problem, you'd rather pray and "bind" the devil for even attempting to influence your significant other. I mean, let's face it. It simply *has* to be the result of the devil and his demons, right? The real reason couldn't possibly be that you have failed to communicate properly or that maybe, just maybe, you're contributing to the strife in your home. And when finances seem to wither? Well, that must be an attack of the devil also, right? Because, let's face it; the real reason could not possibly be that you haven't budgeted well or invested wisely – or that you have still refused to start your own business the way you've talked about for years. It simply *has* to be an attack of the enemy right? And the automobile accident that happened that time? Well, that was simply the demons of Hell attempting to destroy you, correct? In no way was it because you were texting while driving or failing to be more observant, right? And the sickness and fatigue that seems to always plague you? Surely *that* is the enemy attacking you, right? It couldn't possibly be the result of a lack of exercise or poor dietary choices. Everything that feels bad is the result of some attack, right? Although I say such things in no way to make light of the very real ills of the world that we sometimes find ourselves experiencing, I share that to simply highlight the erroneous and, well, "lazy" mindset of spiritual warfare.

Just like literal warfare, though, spiritual warfare is equally if not even more deadly. Like literal war, spiritual warfare brings with it very real casualties – very real deaths. I'm referring to the countless, countless millions upon millions of lives throughout the centuries never able to enjoy abundance or purpose or destiny, that, instead, lived years battling attack after attack – always blaming someone or some "thing" else for their many, varied hardships. There is a very real reason, you see, why the first epistle of Peter makes mention of the enemy seeking to devour and to destroy. *"Be sober, be vigilant; because your adversary the devil, as a roaring lion, walketh about, seeking whom he may devour." (1 Peter 5:8 KJV)* Unlike literal, physical war, though, spiritual warfare is actually much, much more deadly – much more sinister, in fact. Unlike literal, physical wars, which have moments of surrender in sight, spiritual warfare can often be generational and ongoing in nature. Just imagine it, for a moment. "I'm a prayer warrior just like my mother and grandmother before me." "I'm called to the same deliverance ministry as my grandfather." Or, picture this. "The enemy has always attacked my family for as long as I can remember. My grandmother fought cancer and so did my mother." And on and on it goes. At what point, if ever, are you going to finally, once and for all say, "No more!"

For as long as I live, I'll never forget Jacklyn. I met her at a prophetic conference I was ministering at in New York in 2008. Jacklyn had just recently been introduced to the world of "Spirit-filled" believers and had recently begun attending a large charismatic church in the downtown area of the city. Having been passionate about the things of GOD from a very early age and having been hungry to experience the miraculous and the supernatural for as long as she could remember, the baptism of the Holy Spirit changed quite literally everything for Jacklyn. Yet, with the newfound openness to the Spirit, coupled with a newfound church and a newfound belief system, came also the teaching regarding spiritual warfare. Jacklyn remained faithful to her church and even more faithful to what she referred to as her "revelations" about prayer. Four times each week, like clockwork, she would meet a group of intercessors at her church and the group would pray for hours on end, binding and rebuking the enemy over the church and over their respective families. And, daily, in Jacklyn's own, personal life, the war raged on. Waking early each morning, Jacklyn would often spend hours "Pleading the Blood" over her newborn daughter, rebuking any potential sickness that might come, although the doctors continually informed her that her newborn daughter was the picture of perfect health. Often for hours each day, Jacklyn would recite the ninety-first chapter of the Book of Psalms – she knew it by heart. As Jacklyn expressed to me when I met her, it was "exhausting." "I love my faith," she explained to me. "But I don't know how much more I can give." I could see the pain I her eyes. Rather than sensing the force of spiritual power, I sensed within her nothing but drainage and utter and complete emptiness. Jacklyn, you see, had given literally everything and rather than finding herself lifted up, she was being destroyed from within and paralyzed by crippling, irrational fears.

When she approached me, after the conference had ended, she asked, "How can I find peace? It's such a constant battle every day." To this day I can still so vividly remember the response the Holy Spirit gave. Under the unction and inspiration of the Holy Ghost, I said to Jacklyn, simply, "It's alright to change your mind." Those words, still, resonate within me to this day. And to you, my dear friend, I feel inspired to say the same thing. "It's alright to change your mind." Continued dedication to a cause that continues to drain the life out of you is in no way to be considered "faithfulness." Rather, it is "foolishness." You, perhaps, have heard the term "foolishness" defined as doing the same thing over and over again, expecting different results each time. Well, it's true. For generations you and I have been taught to believe that we have no choice in matters regarding spiritual warfare – that life is just destined to be a never ending series of attacks, struggles, and hardships. We've believed that, genuinely. Perhaps you still do. Perhaps, for you, spiritual warfare has become a chief cornerstone of your life as each day you awaken you find yourself living with fear, continuing to attract into your life even more of what you don't want rather than what you truly do want. That can change today, my friend. As I've said for years in ministry, if you truly want to change your life, you begin by changing your thoughts.

If you now find yourself living a life filled with what seems to be constant struggle, daily facing a barrage of attack after attack, I would ask you, simply, "What are you thinking?" Whatever your belief, regardless of your faith, and, above all, no matter what you've been led or taught to believe, it's alright to begin to change your mind. I would ask you, respectfully, is your life becoming better because of what you believe, or is it becoming worse? How does it truly *feel* to believe what you believe? Is the belief providing you with a sense of victory, or are you, rather, experiencing even more attacks, even more hardship, and even more continued daily struggle? What if I were to tell you that you are experiencing each and every day *exactly* what you believe in? Would you find that insulting? Would you view such a claim as nothing more than some heresy? In order for the religious mindset based upon unbiblical ideas to be dismantled and destroyed, it must first be confronted. And so, knowing that, I say with all respect to you that the reason you continue to face constant struggle and constant hardship, always seemingly encountering hardship after hardship is, quite simply, because your religious beliefs aren't working for you. In fact, the truth of the matter is they're killing you. They're keeping you from living an abundant life and, as a result, they're leading you to continue to waste your time on ideas and concepts that are simply not successful.

Often times, I find myself asked by my readers, students, and clients, and audience members whether or not spiritual warfare is real. I always respond by saying, "Yes, in fact, spiritual warfare is very real; but it doesn't have to be." Many respond with a look of being perplexed, wondering what could possibly be meant by such a statement. The answer, though, comes from the very words of Jesus. *"For verily I say unto you, That whosoever shall say unto this mountain, Be thou removed, and be thou cast into the sea; and shall not doubt in his heart, but shall believe that those things which he saith shall come to pass; he shall have whatsoever he saith." (Mark 11:23 KJV)* This account within the scriptures is quite often used to denote the power of prayer and the power residing within the proclamations we decree. However, in truth, the true power of this teaching goes far, far beyond even the power of our own spoken words. In this emphatic declaration, Jesus is reminding us that we will have exactly what we truly believe. Ponder the meaning of such a truth for a moment. In other words, right now, in this exact moment, you and I are experiencing within our lives exactly what we believe in. Show me a life, and, without fail, I will show you a belief. If within your life you are experiencing hardship and struggle, it is simply a reflection of what you are choosing to believe. And, on the contrary, if you are experiencing abundance and peace and joy, it is because you are choosing to believe in those things. I simply cannot stress enough the importance of recognizing that contrary to what you've been told, or taught, or led to believe, it actually is alright to change your mind when you begin to discover that your beliefs are no longer serving you.

Hiroo Onodo continued to fight a war that had ended long, long before he truly accepted it. In many ways, it is much the same with teachings regarding spiritual warfare. You believe in and participate in spiritual warfare simply because you've been told, or taught, or led to believe that it's your duty as a believer to do so. However, it is not. As you will soon see and begin to realize, not only is the very premise of spiritual warfare based upon erroneous and unbiblical teachings but that not once in the entirety of the scriptures will you ever find one account in which even the confrontation with an enemy wasn't based entirely and completely upon a deeply-held, ingrained belief. For years, perhaps even for most of your life, you've lived a life of constant warfare, always seeking to place blame upon someone – or something – else. As a result, you've unknowingly and inadvertently chosen to view your life as a victim rather than as the Creator that you are and have always been. Not only are you a co-creator with GOD, as the scriptures teach, but you have, in fact, always been the Creator within this earth realm, as you will soon begin to see. You will have exactly what you believe.

Recently, I released a book which subsequently became an international bestseller. The book is entitled *Prayer: Think Without Ceasing.* In what I truly believe to be the very first of its kind, the book examines the role our thoughts play within all of our prayers, revealing that our very thoughts, in fact, *are* our prayers. Right now, not only are you experiencing the very real and very tangible results of what you believe, even more so you are experiencing the very result of each and every passing thought you choose to entertain. Oh, how powerful and how marvelous is the mind of Christ within us that we possess the ability to create the lives we truly desire! To say that thoughts become things and that our every belief manifests before our eyes is not some magical or mystical concept. Rather, it is the principle of the Law of Attraction established in the very beginning of Creation when the Creator infused within man the ability to create. As you will soon see, literally every passing thought is infused with the divine intention of the Creator. What you meditate upon, you will continue to attract. What you dwell upon will continue to manifest. To say it another way, when you focus upon war you will attract even more war. When you meditate upon battle and conflict, you will attract only more of the same. And when you dwell upon images of dragons and darkness you will experience your beliefs. The choice, though, is entirely your own. Regardless of your belief and regardless of what you choose to meditate upon, I assure you that the elements of war and struggle are unnecessary within a life within the Kingdom. Truly, the war is over the moment you can finally bring yourself to believe it.

IMAGES AND IDOLS

"Dismantle the ideas that are no longer serving you." – Jeremy Lopez

All throughout the entirety of the scriptures, we are continuously reminded that there is a very real, very intricate correlation between what we believe in and what we see. Exactly 117 times throughout the passages of scriptures, the Holy Bible makes mention of "high places"and the importance of tearing them down. As the children of Israel moved toward the land promised them by GOD, they marched toward a new, strange, and every unfamiliar world – a new world whose customs and beliefs were vastly different from their own. Before ever even crossing Jordan, though, to possess the new land of promise, very specific instructions were given concerning how to deal with idols. The "high places" referenced were areas within the new land of Canaan which had been devoted to the worship of pagan deities. In Numbers chapter thirty-three, an account is depicted in which Moses exhorts the children of Israel to completely tear down and to demolish every such "high place" without exception. *"Then ye shall drive out all the inhabitants of the land from before you, and destroy all their pictures, and destroy all their molten images, and quite pluck down all their high places: And ye shall dispossess the inhabitants of the land, and dwell therein: for I have given you the land to possess it. And ye shall divide the land by lot for an inheritance among your families: and to the more ye shall give the more inheritance, and to the fewer ye shall give the less inheritance: every man's inheritance shall be in the place where his lot falleth; according to the tribes of your fathers ye shall inherit. But if ye will not drive out the inhabitants of the land from before you; then it shall come to pass, that those which ye let remain of them shall be pricks in your eyes, and thorns in your sides, and shall vex you in the land wherein ye dwell." (Number 33:52-55 KJV)*

The command to tear down these "high places" of idol worship served a two-fold purpose. Firstly, the LORD had already commanded that no graven images or false gods be worshipped. Secondly, though, Moses knew instinctively that if these "high places" were to remain intact and left standing, the children of Israel would begin to allow the new and different beliefs of Canaan to influence them. At the time of the migration, there were twenty-six pagan deities being worshipped by the Canaanites, including El, Baal, Ashtoreth, and Dagon. For the children of Israel, these "idols" represented the imagery of hindering, limiting beliefs. When we speak of spiritual warfare, though, reference to these "high places" also serves as a reminder to us of the power resting behind our very own beliefs. I often wonder, for those of that time practicing idolatry and worshipping the graves images, how did they know what their supposed "gods" and "goddesses" looked like? In other words, to put it another way, how did the Canaanites know what the images should resemble? What served as their points of references when crafting such idols? How would they have known to craft the idol devoted to Dagon in one way, while crafting the idol devoted to Ashtoreth another way? The answer is that they simply relied upon their imaginations and their own visualizations. In other worlds, to put it quite simply, the Canaanites had decided what to worship, how to worship, what their deities were to be named, and, also, how their deities were to look. Everything was left to their own interpretation and to their own imaginations.

And now, let us look to this present, current time within humanity, particularly where religious beliefs are concerned. The truth of the matter is that not much has changed. Although, today, within the faith of Christianity, most would never even contemplate bowing down before carved images and idols representing strange, pagan deities, there are "high places" that you are unknowingly yet willingly choosing to bow to each and every day of your life. These "high places," for you, are the "images" connected to your belief system. We all have them, even though we are not always consciously aware of their presence within our lives. These "high places" – these idols – are the images associated with our beliefs and, much like those dwelling within the land of Canaan, these beliefs are the result of our traditions, our customs, our own religious rituals, and, above all, our own interpretations based upon our own thoughts and imaginations.

Whether you realize it yet or not, the reason you continue to face spiritual warfare in your life is because you have allowed your religious customs, your religious tradition, and, yes, even your own imagination to have the final say in the matter rather than being led by the Spirit of truth and relying upon the voice of the inner Kingdom.

These "idols" are the beliefs that you seem to cling to without fail and without question. These beliefs are, as a result, the basis of every action, every passing thought, and every decision you make. Whenever I see genuine and sincere men and women faith boldly preaching their beliefs to others, I often can't help but question, "Do you truly love GOD, or do you simply love your beliefs *about* GOD?" And for those who practice daily spiritual warfare, I would ask, with great respect, "Are you truly warring against the enemy, or are you warring against what your religious beliefs have told you about the enemy?" The answer may surprise you. In other words, you see there has always been and, even still, continues to be a very real and very direct correlation among what we believe and what we see. For far too long, whether you've realized it, consciously, or not, you've crafted an idol – an image – based upon your beliefs. We have all been guilty of this, as it seems intrinsic to human nature the innate need to personify our beliefs. Religion, though, for the most part has only served to strengthen these idols and these internal visual "images" rather than tear them down. And so, as a result, everything that feels unpleasant or unwanted or uncomfortable, to us, automatically becomes the work of some "enemy," as we personify our own emotions and project onto the universe our very own beliefs.

Recognizing this, is it truly any wonder why Jesus said, quite emphatically, that religious traditions make the Word of GOD powerless?

"Making the word of God of none effect through your tradition, which ye have delivered: and many such like things do ye." (Mark 7:13 KJV) The synoptic gospel of Matthew depicts this principle in an even different, more unique way, by stating the miraculous could not happen because of unbelief. *"And he did not many mighty works there because of their unbelief." (Matthew 13:58 KJV)* This passage of scripture has been the basis of many a powerful sermon, message, and teaching regarding the power of belief and the dangers of a lack thereof. However, the truth of the matter is that you and I are always, always, without fail, believing something. And so, to put it another way, within the account contained within the gospel of Matthew, the hindrance came not solely because of a lack of belief but, rather, more specifically because of the presence of very limiting beliefs. You and I encounter these limiting beliefs each and every day of our lives

and have for years. "You're having trouble in your marriage? I'll pray that the enemy will take his hands off your relationship in the name of Jesus." "You didn't get the job promotion you had been wanting? It was the enemy hindering you." And, on the contrary, these very limiting, very hindering beliefs often even define the way in which we view GOD and even our very own selves. "I'm just a sinner saved by grace." "I don't deserve the promotion." "No one could ever really love me." Or, worst of all, perhaps, "Whatever happens happens."

The moment you begin to view yourself as the Creator within your life, just as you were destined to be, never again will you view your life as merely a game of chance or as some roll of the dice. Gone will be the days in which you view yourself and your own life experience as simply the byproduct of some sadistic game of Russian roulette the universe seems to be playing. The universe does not work in that way. Heaven does not work in that way. Furthermore, life within the Kingdom does not have to be lived that way. For years, you've heard it preached and taught that you should not doubt and only believe. For most of your life, perhaps, you've been taught the dangers of unbelief. But what about limiting beliefs? What of all those beliefs which you've held to which simply stopped serving you a long, long time ago, yet you continue to hold to them? These limiting beliefs have become your idol and, with all respect, I must say that whether you've realized it or not, you've allowed many of these limiting, religious beliefs to also become your very own false "god." Sure, it may seem authentic and sincere to spend a life lived in constant battle and spiritual warfare; however, it is actually false humility and pride. It is arrogance and the height of all hypocrisy.

Everything you have within your life today, you have because you have attracted those things into your life based entirely upon the beliefs you've held to. This is the powerful principle of the heavenly, universal Law of Attraction. What you dwell upon and what you continue to focus upon, you will continue to manifest. Proverbs 23:7 declares that we actually become whatsoever we think. And so if you now find yourself living a life which seems unsatisfying and draining – if you now find yourself experiencing a life that seems, well, anything but abundant – it's because of your own limiting beliefs. The issue, in fact, has never been the enemy. No. Instead, the issue has always been, rather, what you believe about the enemy. For that matter, the issue has never been GOD. The issue, instead, has been what you believe about GOD. Above all, the issue has always been what you choose to believe about your very own self. There is a very real adversary, yes. And that adversary has always been your very own limiting belief and lack of understanding of who you truly are, who were always destined to be, and, above all, what you have the power to accomplish. I've always found it rather remarkable and, well, somewhat comical in fact, that in the very beginning within the account of Creation in Genesis the "enemy" appears as a serpent, only to in the Book of Revelation be depicted as a mighty dragon. Have you ever wondered why? Could it be because what we choose to focus upon and choose to give place to grows? The Apostle Paul in his epistle to the church at Ephesus admonishes the church to refrain from "giving place" to the devil. Why? Because what you give place to – what you choose to dwell upon and give your attention to – will continue to manifest. In other words, to put it even more plainly, if you're tired of being attacked, tired of fighting spiritual warfare on a constant, daily basis, and tired of feeling so victimized, change your beliefs, change your mind, and stop dwelling so much on your adversary and begin to focus, instead, on what you do want.

I assure you, my friend, if you would begin to place as much focus – as much meditation – upon the things that you actually do what as you've been placing into battling against what you don't want, your entire life will change in one, instantaneous, miraculous moment. What are you giving place to? That is to say, rather, what are you meditating upon? Rather than warring against what might happen, what feels bad, and what seems to be so very negative, dark, and destructive, why not choose instead to dwell upon what you truly desire? I sense you asking, "Jeremy, are you seeking to insinuate that there is no real enemy?" What I'm saying, dear friend, quite simply, is that how you choose to define your enemy is irrelevant – whether you view your enemy as some horned being wielding a pitchfork, some dark, malevolent entity, some massive, fire-breathing dragon, or even as the "tooth fairy," it makes no difference to me. The single, greatest issue keeping you locked and paralyzed within a life of constant struggle and lack is not your enemy; it is what you are choosing to believe about your enemy. And, furthermore, the beliefs that you are allowing to shape the way in which you view your enemy are, in fact, coming from within your very own self. So, to put it more plainly, your only true adversary is your very own self. Regardless of the definitions, regardless of the imagery, regardless of the titles, at the most basic level of Creation, you have exactly what you choose to believe in.

Throughout my years in global, prophetic ministry, I've often been asked, "Jeremy, why do you rarely talk about the devil?" I always find myself thinking how outlandish and ridiculous such a question truly is. How absurd! Why would I do that? What would be the point of it? Why even give place to or even begin to entertain a notion that possesses no power? Quite frankly, I find it not only disheartening but also quite disgusting, really, to hear sincere men and women of God devote such time and such careful study to such a thing! Is it truly any wonder why much of the church finds itself engaging in daily spiritual warfare? Simply look at what is being preached within the church to understand why! You will manifest and will bring into your life exactly what you believe. Furthermore, because it is from the abundance of the heart that we even speak, those who preach and practice spiritual warfare manifest exactly that. It simply cannot be said enough that you and I will have exactly what we believe. If you desire a life of abundance and peace, begin, first, by dismantling the beliefs that are no longer serving you. Stop dwelling on them!

"Finally, brethren, whatsoever things are true, whatsoever things are honest, whatsoever

things are just, whatsoever things are pure, whatsoever things are lovely, whatsoever things are of good report; if there be any virtue, and if there be any praise, think on these things." *(Philippians 4:8 KJV)* Rather than focusing upon battling against sickness, why not choose, instead, to focus upon health and wellness? Rather than dwelling upon lack, choose abundance instead. Rather than focusing upon loneliness and isolationism, why not choose, instead, to dwell upon the relationships you truly desire? The moment – in fact, the very second – you begin to shift your prayer and meditations and your mindfulness from what you don't want toward what you truly desire, you will begin to see your desires manifest before your very eyes. When the Holy Spirit quickened my mind and awakened me to the truth of this revelation all those years ago, literally everything changed for me within a period of one, single day. When I stopped rebuking the enemy and began to choose, instead, to meditate and to ponder the abundant life I had been promised, I began to see that abundant life manifest all around me. Suddenly, seemingly supernaturally, relationships changed. I began to walk in wellness and wholeness in every area of my life. My finances changed. The ministry was taken to a global audience. And most importantly, above all, I began to live a life that truly felt good.

I often remind people just how important feelings are. Your emotions are a gift, regardless of how they feel. I often think of emotion as the universal indicator or gauge of the abundant life. When the Creator looked upon the handiwork of His craftsmanship, He declared, "It is good." Can you say the same about your life? How does your life feel to you? Truly. What about your faith and your beliefs? Are they satisfying to you? Do they encourage you and inspire you? Do your beliefs cause you to desire more of the things of the Spirit, propelling you into greater, even deeper revelation? Or, on the contrary, do your beliefs cause fear and paranoia? Do your beliefs keep you awake at night? Do your beliefs cause you to dread the unknown and plague you with a sense of doom? If so, then change them. If so, then your religion has lied to you and you've chosen to believe it.

LIFE AND DEATH

"You will attract life, or you will attract death. Choose life." – Jeremy Lopez

When the Holy Spirit first began to quicken my spirit and awaken me to the revelation of the universal Law of Attraction decades ago, it was as if a veil had been lifted. The scriptures and the sacred text of the Holy Bible began to become alive in fresh and revitalizing ways as never before, and for the first time ever, I was able to see that the message of the Kingdom of Heaven is a message of creative force. You and I, as divine and powerful thinking spirits having been infused with the very nature of the Godhead are constantly being given the opportunity with each passing thought to create the lives of our desires. We have been given choice in all things. With the unlimited force of Creation coursing through us, though, comes also the very inconvenient truth that all choices have consequences. For every choice, there comes reaction and manifestation. Contrary to what you and I have been led and taught to believe for years, not even our faith can deliver us from the consequences of our own choices. This is why within the Kingdom there exists a very real and very tangible sense of personal responsibility.

Yes, it would be true to say that because of Christ you and I are co-creators with GOD. However, the greater truth of the matter is that because of the very divine nature that we possess, we are actually Creators within the earth realm, possessing the very creative power of the Godhead, having been given absolute dominion over the spheres of our existence within this physical plane of earth. The scriptures are replete with the theme of

Creation. In the very beginning, as the breath of life was breathed into the newly formed man, man became a living soul. And, in an instant, the very essence of creative power became incarnated – encapsulated into human form. Is it any wonder, really, that the Creator then decreed man would have absolute dominion over the newly formed earth realm? Possessing all the characteristics and the attributes of the Godhead, having been crafted within His image and likeness, man had absolutely no choice but to create. The nature of the Godhead was now the nature of man. And it continues to be so, even now to this very day.

Contrary to the erroneous lies of man-made religions, crafted from the illusionary, false ideas of separation and dichotomy, you and I have never been as depraved and as without hope as we have for so long been led to believe. In spite of what our traditions have taught us, never was there truly a time in which we had ever really fallen from good graces. Yes, a very real "fall" did occur. However, the fall took place within the mind of man and never within the heart of the Creator. When the illusion of separation came and when the mind of man became awakened to a "sin" consciousness, there quickly manifested in the new world a sense of shame and guilt. The man and the woman hid, for the very first time feeling overwhelmed with a strange and bizarre feeling of separation. Even then, though, the Creator came to walk with them in the cool of the day within the garden paradise, just as He always had before. The "fall," as the story goes, mandated that the man and the woman be banished from the newly formed paradise, reminding us that every choice has a consequence. Even in the very beginning, within the account of Creation as depicted within Genesis, we are shown the importance of accepting personal responsibility for our choices.

What we so often fail to realize, though, is that though the mind of man had changed, the true nature of man – that of Creator – never did. This is why long, long after, when the fullness of time had come, there would be another Adam – a second Adam – boldly preaching and proclaiming the truth of the Kingdom. This Adam reminded humanity that the glory had never really departed and that the Kingdom existed within all. In the beginning of it all, in the garden paradise all those generations prior, the idea of "war" was nonexistent. How could there be war when there was only the identity of Oneness with the Godhead? There was no religion then. There was no spiritual warfare. There was no need for such things because there was no illusion of separation. Man did not regard himself as a depraved, fallen soul. Rather, man was reminded, daily, of his own creative power. Yet, when the second Adam came in the fullness of time, when the Word, again, became encapsulated into human flesh, this second Adam found himself in a world that seemed much, much different from the original garden home. In *this* world, there was religion – Pharisees and Sadducees who confronted him at every turn. There were what seemed to be very dark and very sinister forces at work. There was sickness. There was disease. There were those oppressed by demons – some even fully possessed. The world of the second Adam seemed so very different. It seemed that so much had changed.

I share this with you in this way, my friend, to better illustrate the very real and very lasting consequences that always accompany the choices we make. As you can see, a lot can change when we begin to believe wrong things about ourselves and about GOD. Wrong belief and limiting belief makes us prone to even more limiting belief, as a sort of self-fulfilling prophecy becomes enacted. The entire time, because of our unlimited and sovereign nature as Creator, we attract even more of what we choose to believe. And on and on it goes, really. I feel impressed by the Holy Spirit to remind you of who you truly are and of who you always have been. You are not merely a co-creator with GOD. No. Rather, you are a Creator within this earth realm. And, even now, you are attracting into your life – creating – exactly what you believe. The issue you now find yourself facing, though, is that for far too long you've believed the wrong thing about GOD and about yourself. And as a result, you have attracted into your life the need for "war." All because you've believed you've needed to. You've attracted sickness by believing that sickness is just a necessary evil. You've waged war against demons, the devil, and the darkness, all because you've been led to believe that a "fallen" world is controlled by such things. I would remind you, though, just as Jesus did throughout his earthly life and ministry, it doesn't have to be this way. You don't have to believe the wrong things. You still possess the power to change your mind.

Belief is the most powerful force in existence because, quite literally, we possess the thoughts of a Creator. This is why to better understand the true power of life within the Kingdom we must understand the universal Law of Attraction and the heavenly Law of Creation. You and I, by divine and intelligent design, are constantly, day by day, attracting into our lives the very things we meditate upon. With each passing thought, the spark of creative force is ignited, with each flicker becoming magnetized. Religion would much rather have you believe that all of the negative – all of the struggle – exists as punishment for a "fall." It's easier that way, you see. It's always been much easier to blame others and to personify our fears. It's much easier, you see, to say, "The devil made me do it" than it is to admit, "I'm causing this because of my wrong and limiting beliefs." Personal responsibility is often a bitter pill to swallow. And so we would much rather seek to take up the cross of Jesus in an attempt to alleviate ourselves from the burden of responsibility – the entire time that Jesus commanded that we take up our very own crosses before following him. This is the impetus of personal responsibility. As the old adage goes, with great power comes great responsibility. It really is true, though. Right now, today, you are once again being given a choice. You are given a choice by being asked in each and in every passing moment, "Are my beliefs working?"

"And if it seem evil unto you to serve the Lord, choose you this day whom ye will serve; whether the gods which your fathers served that

were on the other side of the flood, or the gods of the Amorites, in whose land ye dwell: but as for me and my house, we will serve the Lord." (Joshua 24:15) You see, my friend, it doesn't have to be the way it's always been. You don't have to cling to the same beliefs as you your father, your mother, or your grandparents, or of all those who have come before. This is a brand new day, and what once may have well worked in other times passed no longer works. To put it another way, allow me to say it in this way. Just because your mother and father struggled and faced hardship doesn't mean that it has to be the same for you. Yes, we honor their faith, and we honor their commitment; however, the experience of your own life is not based upon the beliefs of others. You are solely and singularly responsible for the Creation within your own sphere of life – your own, personal "metron." There is no one else to blame, as difficult as it may be to accept.

As a lifelong student of the scriptures and seeker, I've always found it fascinating the accounts contained within the synoptic gospels that depict Jesus dealing with darkness and the "demonic." Centuries later, based upon the text and the accounts, entire teachings have been developed within the charismatic movement which detail steps for successful "spiritual warfare." All throughout the accounts in the gospels, though, never once do we see "spiritual warfare." There was never any fight – any true "war" – when dealing with darkness. With a single word demons were driven out. There was no struggle. There was no fear that the confrontation might somehow fail. No. There was only the utter and complete, absolute knowledge that darkness and light cannot coexist. In Matthew chapter seventeen and in Mark chapter nine, we are shown an account in which the disciples find themselves unable to cast out demons. For them, there was confrontation and struggle. For Jesus, though, there was no struggle. He simply gave the word. These accounts reveal to us, perhaps more than all others, not only the power of belief but also the damaging dangers of limiting and wrong beliefs.

What if I told you that you continue to suffer attack after attack and face what seems to be the constant barrage of darkness and negativity solely, simply because you are continuing to dwell upon it? What if I told you that with every passing moment, you've been given the choice to either dwell on and to meditate upon either what you do not want or upon what you do want? Would such a statement be offensive to the religious, natural mind? Imagine how incredibly freeing it would be to recognize that you possess the power to not only change the spiritual atmosphere around you but also possess the power to reshape, to mold, and to craft the physical elements of your life to your liking based entirely upon your own beliefs. This is the true power of the Creator. And you and I are the Creator within this earth realm. For far too long, you've lived life with the false and erroneous assumption that in a "fallen" world, having fallen from good graces you have absolutely no choice but to simply "endure" until it all gets better. I would ask, though, with all respect, how is that believe truly working for you? Is it satisfying to you? Or is it draining the very life force from you on a daily basis and only serving to fuel and to heighten the sense of fear and paranoia as you find yourself feeling victimized? I would dare to suggest that it's, in fact, the latter rather than the former.

"My people are destroyed for lack of knowledge: because thou hast rejected knowledge, I will also reject thee, that thou shalt be no priest to me: seeing thou hast forgotten the law of thy God, I will also forget thy children." *(Hosea 4:6 KJV)* A lack of

knowledge leads to destruction. To put it another way, limiting, wrong beliefs lead to suffering and calamity. The Word of the LORD through the prophet Hosea serves also as a reminder to us that wrong thinking and limiting, wrong beliefs can have long-lasting, generational consequences. How much of your hardship has been generational in nature, all because you were led to believe or taught to believe that struggle and hardship are necessary evils in life? My friend, I would say to you through the unction of the Holy Spirit, the struggles and the hardships of past generations before you do not have to continue to be your hardships and your struggles. For far too long, you've taken ownership of the limiting and erroneous religious lies of the past and you've allowed them to influence and to dictate your thinking in your own daily life. It's time to make another choice. It's time to choose again!

In each and every passing moment, because you possess the nature of Creator, you are being given the choice to dwell either upon what you do not want or upon what you truly desire. Because of the heavenly Law of Attraction and the divine, universal Law of Creation, you are constantly creating something. You have no choice in the matter. You are continuing to fully manifest your beliefs based entirely upon the choice you make. Which thoughts have you been focusing and meditating upon? Have you found yourself focusing upon the things you do not want, rather than upon the life you truly desire? Today is the day to make another choice. Begin to choose life! Rather than praying against the sickness that you do not want and constantly, daily, rebuking enemies and casting down dark forces around you, why not simply begin to focus on health? Why not begin to focus and meditate upon abundance? Why not begin to dwell upon the many wonderful relationships existing all around you? Why not begin to, rather than see yourself as some fallen, depraved human, begin to see yourself the way you truly are? Stop living beneath your means. Begin to choose life rather than   death!

AWAKENINGS

"Every revelation will be tested." – Jeremy Lopez

Throughout the course of human history, humanity has seen moments of great awakening – seasons in which the divine revelations of the Spirit have been proclaimed throughout each and every passing generation that has ever walked upon the earth. With revelation, though, always comes a time of great testing. So often, as we look to the past and see these defining moments and seasons, we often refer to them as "moves" of GOD. Personally and prophetically speaking, I do not believe in alternate and different "moves" of God, as much I believe that in each and every generation there comes moments of awakening in which revelations are proclaimed and made popular. Throughout history, these seasons of awakening have been "revivals" and "renewals." Regardless of the terms we choose to use, though, throughout history we have seen moments in which new and exciting revelations have been shared with the world for the cause of Christ. From the first and second "Great Awakening," to the resurgence of Pentecost, to the charismatic renewal which gave rise to the great healing evangelists of the 1950's and the 1960's, to the more recent periods referred to as times of "outpouring" at Brownsville, at Toronto, at Lakeland, periods of time have come in which new and exciting revelations have been shared.

With the good, though, has also, at times, come the confusion, as many genuine and sincere men and women of genuine and sincere faith have run headlong into strange and seemingly bizarre doctrines having no basis in biblical, scriptural, or theological truth. Often times, in the midst of genuine excitement, unbiblical beliefs are turned into doctrines of the faith, all under the guise of "new revelation." Not only is such a rush to judgement dangerous; often times such a rush is quite deadly. In the midst of the charismatic renewal, particularly within the 1980's, there began to be talk of "spiritual warfare." With the rise of the so-called "new revelation" came, also, popular teachings, countless books upon the subject, and courses on demonology, as many sincere men and women of faith found themselves thrust headlong in all-out "war." Prophetically speaking, though, the great pendulum of history is always swinging – moving to the extreme left and to the extreme right. In the midst of all the extreme, though, somewhere in the midst of the movement of it all, lies the truth of sound, biblical doctrine.

The charismatic movement, which helped to fuel the flames of the teachings regarding spiritual warfare, changed everything it seemed. Going far beyond doctrines of healing or even doctrines concerning prophecy, the movement of spiritual warfare began to encourage audiences around the globe to begin to become more acquainted and more familiar with the "enemy." In spiritual warfare, literally everything unpleasant or unwanted suddenly became the work of "demons" or the "devil." As intense the fervor and as seemingly heavenly the newfound revelation, there were flaws. Damage was being done in the name of the new revelation, as many flocked toward the teaching without ever really testing it. What I do absolutely know from decades of prophetic ministry is that every so-called "revelation" will be tested. When tested, some will withstand the test of time and others will simply vanish away into obscurity, onto the ash heap of Christian history. What happens, though, when we continue to cling to teachings that have not been tried or tested? What are the results? What are the consequences? Confusion begins to abound, as we begin to build our lives around emotion and frenzy, rather than remaining grounded upon biblical truth within the Kingdom. In truth, for all the good that has at times come from the teachings regarding spiritual warfare, I dare say that much more damage has been done.

Sincere men and women were taught to fear. And many of them, in fact, are even now struggling to find some sense of normalcy within their own, daily lives as they continue to look for "demons" at every turn and continue to fail to take personal responsibility for their own lives and actions. Spiritual warfare could very well be one of the most damnable and erroneous lies religion has ever invented, though – far, far worse than most others because it teaches us to cast blame onto others while neglecting to take personal responsibility for our very own lives. Spiritual warfare, you see, promotes and praises the "enemy" rather than proclaiming the creative and sovereign power of the inner Kingdom which Jesus spoke of. In order to begin to dismantle and to destroy unbiblical beliefs, though, requires first confronting those erroneous teachings. As I write this, even now, I find myself reminded of the story of John. Though I'm not referring to John the Revelator, like the Apostle John, this John I'm speaking of was also in ministry and had just received a "revelation" when I first met him.

John was new to charismatic ministry when I first met him. After attending a prophetic conference in his city, John had been introduced to the concept of spiritual warfare. Although he had been a believer for decades before, there was something about the new revelation of spiritual warfare that sparked his interest. Before long, John found himself immersed in teachings regarding the "enemy," "demons," and forces of darkness. Although John had for years lived in such joy and peace, before long he found himself feeling led to constantly fight against and rebuke, well, literally anything and everything that he didn't want in his life. Before long, the new revelation he had received even began to affect his marriage and his family. "He had always been so understanding before all this," his wife said. "Now, whenever we have a disagreement he blames the devil for it." It had begun to affect the intimacy of the marriage and even the communication. "Instead of having conversations and trying to understand each other, he tells me that I'm being influenced by the enemy and not submitting to spiritual authority if I disagree with him," his wife Katie said. Within only a matter of weeks, everything changed. What had begun as a very real and very sincere faith had quickly devolved into frenzy, fear, paranoia, and what some might even consider being a form of psychosis. The change was so stark and so abrupt that it seemed to be a literal break from reality.

John was at risk of losing his wonderful wife and children. When he spoke to his "mentor," though, the man who had taught him about spiritual warfare and deliverance ministry, John was told, quite simply, "Your wife is being used by the enemy to cause confusion for you." And on and on it went. Before long, John found himself unable to sleep. Where he had once had nights spent in perfect peace, he now found himself plagued by tormenting nightmares. In dreams, he would see his wife killed tragically in automobile accidents. He would awaken to see terrifying visions and what seemed to be dark, shadowy silhouettes lining the walls of his bedroom. To John, though, this was all merely the further attacks of the enemy, happening to deter him from pursuing his ministry as an intercessor. Ultimately, even John's health began to deteriorate. When I met John, he was simply a shell of his former self – alone, divorced, battling a rare blood disease, and teetering on the verge of collapse after having filed bankruptcy. Everything that John had fought against had come upon him. To his mentors and fellow intercessors, though, the struggle was warranted. The hardships, from their perspective, served as confirmation that John was simply paying the price for his strong faith. When John came to the offices of Identity Network on that warm April day, I immediately sensed the spirit of death around him. It was as if the moment he walked into the room, a dark, shadowy cloud followed him. Rather than emanating the bright light of the Kingdom, he exuded only darkness and depression. He had already lost so much. I sensed by the Holy Spirit that if something did not change immediately, there would be absolute destruction soon.

As I listened to John share with me his beliefs and talk about his calling into intercession and spiritual warfare, I could not help but feel his immense pain. I had absolutely no doubt that John was sincere in his beliefs – he was as authentic to his beliefs as is humanly possible. However, I also knew that if John did not change his mind and evolve from the so-called "revelation" that had been imparted to him, he would not survive much longer. I looked at John and with love, I simply asked, "My friend, why are you worshipping the enemy?" There was an immediate look of bewilderment that came upon John's face. He was shocked by such a question and understandable so. I could feel that he had taken offense to the question posed; however, in total and complete transparency, that was my intention. You see, in order for a religious stronghold to be dismantled, it must first be confronted. He responded, "How could you even ask me that?" In anger, he said defiantly, "I worship Jesus only!" As well-intentioned and as genuine as such a response seemed, though, it simply wasn't true. Rather than focusing upon the goodness, the majesty, and the wonders of the LORD, John had been deceived into focusing, instead, upon the darkness, the enemy and all the wiles of the devil. As a result, John had attracted into his life the very thing he claimed to despise. John's religious belief, though well-intentioned and sincere, was literally killing him. I asked John, lovingly, "If Jesus is LORD of all, then who are you fighting, my friend?" Another look of bewilderment came upon his face. I watched as the dark cloud of depression dissipated and a look of fear and dread became replaced with a smile and with a sense of joy. Within four weeks, John's health improved. He began to find financial success, again, and his marriage was restored.

You see, my friend, there is truly nothing more "demonic" than the unbiblical, erroneous teaching regarding spiritual warfare. It teaches us to focus more upon he enemy than upon enjoying the abundant life and, as well-intentioned as such a teaching may seem, it ultimately only produces more darkness and destruction. It is a universal law of the Kingdom, and there are no exceptions. What you set your focus upon, you give your worship to. And, furthermore, what you meditate upon, you will attract into your life. What you focus upon will expand and will grow until it becomes a reality in your own life. And so, rather than studying your enemy, why not choose, instead, to recognize and remember the power you have been entrusted with as a Creator within the earth realm? Rather than focusing upon the negative, the dark, and the unwanted, why not choose, instead, to focus and to meditate upon the good things of the Kingdom? I assure you, my friend, the very moment you begin to realize that you possess the power to end the war within your own self, the war will, in fact, end. *"Let the words of my mouth, and the meditation of my heart, be acceptable in thy sight, O Lord, my strength, and my redeemer." (Psalms 19:14 KJV)* To say this in another way, the focus of your attention is the object of your worship. What you meditate upon will determine the manifestation you will experience. And so why not allow those thoughts to be pleasing and acceptable thoughts? Why not allow them to be pleasing and acceptable, not only to GOD but also to you?

I've always been fascinated by the way in which Jesus spoke of the darkness. Contrary to what popular religious teachings suggest, he very rarely ever spoke of such things. Perhaps it was because such things do not warrant time or attention. Perhaps it was because he refused to play into the fear and paranoia of humanity. In the synoptic gospel of Matthew, though, we do find one of the few accounts in which Jesus does make mention of the darkness, and his teaching is quite remarkable. *"When the unclean spirit is gone out of a man, he walketh through dry places, seeking rest, and findeth none. Then he saith, I will return into my house from whence I came out; and when he is come, he findeth it empty, swept, and garnished. Then goeth he, and taketh with himself seven other spirits more wicked than himself, and they enter in and dwell there: and the last state of that man is worse than the first. Even so shall it be also unto this wicked generation."* (Matthew 12:43-45 KJV) In this account within the gospel of Matthew, Jesus affirms that what we dwell upon will continue to grow – that it will continue to increase. He reveals to us, quite simply, that what we *choose* to give place to will grow in such a way that it will ultimately overtake us. *This*, my friend, is just another illustrative confirmation of the true power you and I possess as Creators within the earth realm. You and I, by divine design, possess the power to draw into our lives exactly what we focus upon, meditate upon, and continue to ponder. This is why the scriptures remind us to be filled, fully to overflowing with *knowledge. "For this cause we also, since the day we heard it, do not cease to pray for you, and to desire that ye might be filled with the knowledge of his will in all wisdom and spiritual understanding."* (Colossians 1:9 KJV)

My friend, my prayer for you is that by now you are able to realize and to discern that religious teachings and spiritual understanding are in no way synonymous. Not every revelation is beneficial. Not every popular teaching, disguising itself as "Christian" is wholesome. And, for that matter, not every newfound prophetic revelation is even real. The plumb line, though – the gauge by which we can determine what is lasting, what is real, and what is true – is the all-important, all-powerful question: "Is this belief beneficial to me?" Is it leading to greater abundance? Is it leading to more of a sense of peace, of joy, and of contentment? Is it manifesting within your life the very desires of your heart and creating for you a life that truly feels good? Or is it, rather, manifesting and bringing into your life everything that you don't want? You possess the power to choose your thoughts. You possess the things – the beliefs, the images, and the visualizations – that fill your mind. Rather than giving your focus, your meditation and, in turn, your worship to that which you do not want, why not choose, instead, to begin to focus upon the light? Focus upon the illumination of the inner Kingdom within which Jesus spoke of and begin to realize and recognize that in order to possess the abundant life requires focusing upon it? You, today, are being given yet another choice. What life do you truly desire? One of constant struggle, constant lack, and constant warfare or one of peace, joy, love, and contentment?

The teaching of the heavenly, Kingdom Law of Attraction was the basis of my bestselling books *The Universe is at Your command: Vibrating the Creative Side of GOD* and *Creating with Your Thoughts*. When the Holy Spirit began to awaken me all those years ago to the knowledge and understanding of the true creative power we possess as beings crafted within His image, I was changed in an instant, and I felt inspired to share the teaching with the world. Something truly remarkable begins to happen, you see, the very instant – the very moment – that we become awakened to our true identity in Christ. All of the sudden, because of the illuminating light of the Spirit, the cunning and crafty wiles of the enemy begin to seem much, much less impressive. When we become filled with knowledge of His will and illuminated with all spiritual understanding, all of the sudden, in an instant, we begin to not only view spiritual warfare as a waste of time but we also begin to see that the "enemy" truly isn't worthy of even a single, passing thought. Stop giving attention to the very things you know are unsatisfying to you and begin to, instead, dwell upon, meditate upon, and think of the abundant life you so richly deserve. You have been promised a life of abundance within the Kingdom – not a life of hardship, struggle, and lack, filled with day after day waging spiritual wars against ideas and imaginations that were put to death long, long ago.

TRANSFERENCE

"Where attention goes, energy flows." – Jeremy Lopez

When the Spirit began to impress upon me the inspiration for this book, I found myself asking how it might be possible to write a book regarding the elements of spiritual warfare without in any way giving credit to the enemy. Throughout the past, through countless teachings and through countless sermons, many sincere men and women of faith have spoken regarding the subject of spiritual warfare, all the while, not realizing that they were inadvertently glorifying their adversary. As I began to become awakened to the leading of the Spirit concerning how to share this revelation and knowledge which transformed my life and ministry all those years ago, I began to find myself reminded, yet again, of the all-powerful creative "energy" which resides in all our many, different beliefs. And then, in turn, I began to realize that my single, greatest purpose is not to attempt to change what you believe about your enemy. The way in which you view your adversary, in truth, means very little. I hope that by now you're beginning to realize that the main purpose of this powerful revelation is to inspire you to begin to change the way in which you view yourself – and your own beliefs.

Have you ever asked yourself, "Why do I believe what I believe?" Or, even, "When did I start to believe what I believe?" If so, you may have realized that it seemed rather difficult to answer those questions because those answers aren't always easily obtained. Often times, as we go throughout our lives, we become implanted with the seeds of ideas, usually without ever even realizing it really. Before long, though, what started with just a casual conversation in passing or a lesson from a Wednesday night Bible study or a book read becomes such a driving force behind our beliefs, our theology, and our overall worldview. This is why it is so, so very important to be ever-vigilant when guarding and protecting our minds. Whether you realize it or not, consciously speaking, you have allowed yourself to become impregnated with the beliefs, the ideas, and the imaginations of others concerning spiritual warfare. When asking yourself why it is that you believe what you believe, I would dare say that the reason is, quite often, because of the beliefs, the opinions, and the theology of those around you.

When awakening comes, though, and when the illumination of the inner Kingdom begins to shine ever more brightly, the lies begin to become exposed, as we become more able to see beyond the illusions which have for so long clouded our judgements. Jesus made it quite clear, as recounted within the synoptic gospel of John, that when the Spirit comes, we will be led into all truth. Imagine that, would you? Not partial truth. And not religious truth. *"Howbeit when he, the Spirit of truth, is come, he will guide you into all truth: for he shall not speak of himself; but whatsoever he shall hear, that shall he speak: and he will shew you things to come."* *(John 16:13 KJV)* Part of the reason that you seem to continue to struggle each day is because you haven't fully realized that you possess the divine, supernatural ability to filter and to process what you hear. As simple as such a statement may seem, I assure you, part of ending your struggle rests in learning to realize that the belief in the struggle, in part, came from other people.

I often say, "Where attention goes, energy flows." It really is true. It's a very real principle within the Kingdom of Heaven. That is to say, quite simply, the thoughts and the ideas you focus upon will become the beliefs which will shape your life. Right now, in this moment, you and I are experiencing the very real, very tangible results of our beliefs. The life of struggle spent waging wars and the life of abundance and prosperity are both equal, in that they are, both, the result of belief. The outcomes of those lives, though, as you might imagine are completely different. One is filled with drainage and fatigue after having to endure continuous struggle, while the other is enjoyed and lived to the fullest. And so, knowing this, if we are truly the result of our own beliefs as the scriptures make perfectly clear, how important is it that we understand *why* we believe what we believe? In truth, it is absolutely critical. In order to begin to free yourself from your own limited thinking and in order to begin to dismantle unbiblical, erroneous beliefs, you must begin to realize that at some point, long,

long ago, you allowed yourself to take on and to conform to the beliefs of others. By realizing this, you can begin to better understand who it is that you truly are and have always been destined to be.

At the end of the day we are all, equally, striving to do the very best we possibly can with what we know. In that regard, we are all equal, as we all seek to gain greater knowledge and insight. And then, as we begin to learn more and begin to know better, hopefully we begin to, in turn, do better. All belief is not equal though, as the outcomes of beliefs are always quite different. For instance, the belief in prosperity and abundance will lead to a very real outcome while the belief in spiritual warfare will lead to an outcome – both very different in nature. So, in truth, although we are continuously and always being given opportunity after opportunity to *know* better, how often do we find ourselves still holding to the beliefs of the past, clinging to the thoughts, the ideas, and the imaginations of yesteryear, under the guise of faithfulness? Within countless circles within the faith, you've heard this presented to you in another way – as "spiritual authority." Spiritual authority, though very real, has been used as the basis for a great many sins within the faith and has been singlehandedly responsible for countless lives ruined and damaged beyond repair.

"I can't question my pastor; he's my spiritual covering." "The prophet told me to never question." "I'd be in rebellion if I went against the beliefs of my church." My friend, in case you have yet to realize it or not, there's a great big world out there, existing to be explored, enjoyed, and experienced. With nothing but great respect your beliefs and to the men and women of faith you've chosen to surround yourself with, the truth of the matter is that they aren't always right. I've said for years, regarding my own work and my own teachings, if they resonate with you and bring you peace and comfort and lead you into greater truth, then, "Wonderful." If the teachings do no resonate with you, then I wish you peace and love regardless. Never once will you ever see the global ministry of Identity Network try to convince you that we're always right and that our beliefs are superior. I'm just a messenger, but I trust that the Spirit is still well able to lead to all truth. If your pastor, your prophet, a visiting evangelist, some so-called "apostle" or any other teacher attempts to convince you that you do not have the right to question your own beliefs, then, my friend, not only is that person a charlatan, a con-artist, and a liar, but that person is operating with the spirit of antichrist. You have the power and the divine, supernatural ability – and the right – to not only examine what you believe but to also change what you believe, and anyone who tries to hinder you from coming into greater knowledge is operating in manipulation and insecurity rather than prophetic anointing.

Sadly, though, it's often from this place of insecurity and manipulation that some of the most damnable doctrines of Hell have been promoted by religion, all under the guise of "spiritual authority." Usually, when questioned, the answer is typically, "Because I said so." Or, "Just because." If we were to be completely honest, it isn't truly that difficult to see why the false doctrines regarding spiritual warfare have prospered and flourished so wildly throughout the years. There's something innate within the human condition that causes us to want to control, to judge, and to have the final say in the matter, without question. From a sociological and even anthropological perspective, this is where civilizations began, really – groups of people bonding together over shared, common beliefs. And then those shared beliefs create reinforcement and, as time passes, it becomes easy to say, "Our way is the only true way." Before long, why is there even a need to change when everything seems so comfortable and so familiar? Religion also works in this exact way, as groups of people bond together over shared, common thoughts, ideas, and beliefs. The difference with religion, though, is that it also brings with it the mandate of evangelism. "Not only are we right, but if you don't share in the belief then you're wrong."

So I would ask, again, why do you believe what you believe and when did you truly begin to believe it? To better understand this, it is important to delve into what I call the power of "transference." Each and every day, with each passing thought, energy is being moved, shaped, crafted, projected, and internalized. Everything is energy, as science continues to prove to us, reminding us that, as the scriptures have said, everything is being "built," line upon line and precept upon precept. There is always energy. To even read these words requires a very real transference of energy. As I write these words to you, my words are becoming infused with the power of intention as I seek to convey the intended message. And when you read these words, there will be the energy of interpretation, as you either internalize the intention I seek to convey or dismiss it without regard. This "transference" of energy, though, is happening on a daily basis at all times as we go throughout life. It happens through conversation. It can even happen with a single smile, as two strangers pass on the streets. Intention is energy moving and flowing. There is absolutely not one single place in existence where the energy of intention does not always exist.

If you find yourself now reading these words and living a life of constant struggle, always feeling the need to fight, to war against, and to battle, it's because you've allowed yourself to become impregnated with the beliefs of others which seem to suggest that a life of struggle is simply a necessary evil. You've been led to believe that struggle is necessary, well, just "because." You've been impregnated with a belief that seems to say, "GOD wants to bless me but the enemy always wants to stop it." And on and on it goes, as time continues to pass by. My friend, the truth is you and I aren't getting any younger. When do you plan to experience the life of abundance you've been promised? If not today, then when? I feel led to share something with you that I feel will change your life forever, if you'll receive it. You could not be any more like GOD even if you wanted to be. You – that is, the real you – are equally as sovereign and equally as spiritual as the Godhead who infused you with His very own essence. Like Him, you are the Creator within the earth realm and have been given absolutely dominion within your own, daily sphere of influence and experience. The world you experience daily has been given to you for your own good pleasure. Is the life you're living a life that feels "good?" Do your beliefs – the beliefs which serve as the basis of your life experiences – feel "good?" If not, then I would suggest you begin to dismantle the unbiblical, erroneous teachings that you have allowed to take root within your life. Expose them and uproot them.

And now you might find yourself asking, "Why is it even important to know what I believe and why I believe it?" The answer, quite simply, is because the way in which you view GOD, the way in which you view the enemy, the way in which you view the world around you, and, yes, even the way in which you view others are directly determined by the way in which you are choosing to view your very own self and your very own role in the world. My friend, there is either war or peace –

either the light or the dark – and there is no in-between. Your thoughts, though, are the filter through which you interpret the world around you, thereby creating the life you now experience. And so, I would respectfully urge you to become much more awakened – much more aware – of the fact that not every belief has to be internalized. Not every lesson you've heard about spiritual warfare has to be accepted and believed. And, above all, not every teaching about the enemy has to be incorporated into your thoughts, your beliefs, and your theology. It's alright to use the Divine Mind you've been given to begin to filter through and to process the information you've been given. It's alright to dissect, to analyze, to examine, and, yes, even to throw away literally every belief you've formed. It's alright to "reason," as Isaiah reminds us. Not only is this reasoning important, but it is crucial if you are ever going to experience a rich, abundant life, here and now.

"Beloved, when I gave all diligence to write unto you of the common salvation, it was needful for me to write unto you, and exhort you that ye should earnestly contend for the faith which was once delivered unto the saints." *(Jude 1:3 KJV)* The term "contend" quite literally means "to wrestle." Contrary to what you've been told, though, this has nothing to do with wrestling or fighting others, feeling called to become a "demon hunter," to even wrestling against the forces of darkness. Instead, it has quite literally everything to do with wrestling your own self, within your own thoughts to examine your own beliefs. Analyze your own faith. Examine it. Dissect it. Work through it. As you will soon see, by beginning to examine your own beliefs, your own thoughts, and your own imagination, you will, in turn, begin to realize that the greatest adversary has always

been your very own mind and the thoughts that you continue to dwell upon. As you will soon begin to see and to recognize, there are very real, very powerful unseen forces at work around you and within you. These forces, though, are the forces of creative energy emanating from within your very own thoughts.

RESIST AND REPENT

"Stand firm in your faith!"

As I began to ponder the true meaning behind spiritual warfare and as the LORD began to quicken my spirit with this revelation concerning what we believe and what we continue to attract into our lives, I began to realize that it truly isn't difficult to see why the unbiblical and false ideologies of spiritual warfare have become so mainstream throughout the past few decades. We live in an entertainment-based culture that thrives on the theatrical. Don't feel bad about it; we all love theatrics to some degree. We enjoy entertainment, by divine design. When we begin to bring our need for theatrics into our theology, though, a lot can go wrong and confusion can begin to abound. For most of my life, for as long as I can remember, really, I've been a student of the scriptures. Even while working to complete my doctoral dissertation all those years ago, I found myself delving not only into the sacred text of the scriptures but also beginning to more closely examine the great history of our faith. Within each season – each paradigm – of spiritual awakening and renewed zeal for the cause of Christ, history has given rise to various, prominent leaders who have heralded their beliefs – often in the most theatrical of ways. I don't believe in any way that it does a disservice to the tenets of the faith to admit that often times there has been some unnecessary showmanship added. It's alright to admit that, because it's true.

As we think of the many great generals of the faith throughout history, we think of the many great healing evangelists of the past and also of the fiery evangelists who reached global audiences. In many ways we all owe a great debt to all those who have come before us – to all who have in any way helped to aid the cause of Christ throughout the world. However, again, it's alright to admit that a great deal of showmanship and performance has been unnecessarily added to the cause throughout the years as well. In fact, to refuse to admit it is to not only be disingenuous but also to do a great disservice to our heritage of faith. As men and woman of faith throughout the past sought to garner and attract even larger audiences, business were created and ministry organizations were launched, and, quite frankly, very literal "brands" were marketed to the masses. There were some who specialized in healing. There were others who specialized in the prophetic arts. Some specialized in the sharing the history of revival itself. And some, also, used the elements of "deliverance" and "spiritual warfare" to target certain demographics within the faith. Notable pioneers of the faith who come to mind are Smith Wigglesworth, Aimee Semple McPherson, Kathryn Kuhlman, Oral Roberts, and many, many others.

With these great giftings, though, came also the theatrics that almost always accompany the stage and screen. Like me, I'm sure you can still so vividly recall images of many notable leaders upon television screens on Sunday morning telecasts, laying hands upon attendees and with loud voices commanding the demons to "come out." If you know me well then you know my heart is in no way to seek to discredit such things. I simply believe that it's important that we begin to grow in our understanding of spiritual matters – particularly where the element of spiritual warfare is concerned. I often cannot help but wonder, long, long after the television lights were darkened and long, long after the crowded arenas were emptied, how many of those sincere and genuine people of faith were able to continue the joy and the abundance of hope that they were shown in the passionate moments of those crusades? Were they able to go on to live abundant lives because they had been given sacred and deep and lasting truth? Or were there emotions simply exploited and capitalized upon in order to make for interesting and entertaining television? Again, I say that not to in any way attempt to discredit the genuine and the real; I say that because our faith begs the question to be asked. What is true? What is real? What is lasting? And what is simply charlatanism?

As I write this to you, I'm reminded of the passage within the scriptures which gives very simple yet detailed instructions on how to actually confront the enemy. *"Submit yourselves therefore to God. Resist the devil, and he will flee from you." (James 4:7 KJV)* As you can see, within this passage showing us explicitly how we are to confront the "adversary," there is no struggle depicted. There is no battle being waged. There is no battle having to be fought. There is no war. It's simply a matter of resisting. It's remarkable to me, really, how from this an entire theology has been built around the premise of violent, never ending, spiritual warfare, as if to suggest that there must always be some struggle involved. When self-defeating thoughts come, simply ignore them. Nothing more. Nothing less. Remembering that it is the thought we give place to which determines the outcome of our experience, when experiencing the limiting, and self-depreciating elements of negativity, worry, fear, pain, and dread, we are reminded that we possess the power to simply shift our focus onto other things. This is the power that we possess, not only as believers within the Kingdom, but as individuals crafted and formed within the very nature of the Creator.

For a moment, I'd like for you to join me upon a journey within your very own mind. I'd like to ask you a very real, yet simply question, and I want to encourage you to answer the question for yourself, in your very own way – in a way that is sincere and authentic to your very own journey. What is left of your faith, after you strip away the theatrics of it all? If you were to take away the fervor and the frenzy, the fiery, loud charisma, all the music, the stage lights, the designer wardrobes, the stage itself, and even the ministers, what would you have left? Would there even *be* anything left? Answer honestly for yourself, as genuinely and as honestly as you possibly can. After the crowds have left and the auditorium has become darkened till another day – after the very last altar call has been given and after you've placed your money into the offering plate – when you find yourself alone, what's truly left? What are you left to hold to that will sustain you and keep you content? Is there a truth, even then, that is satisfying to you, or do you simply find yourself waiting until the next performance? I ask this because, in truth, it makes no difference to me which church you attend or if you attend at all. It's inconsequential to me what you choose to believe or what you choose to preach. My concern for you, quite simply, is whether or not what you believe is working for you to give you the life you so richly deserve. My sincere and heartfelt prayer is that in the midst of all the showmanship, the theatrics, and the performance that you are able to have a belief that truly works to provide you with all that you've been promised.

What happens when the noise ends and you find yourself in silence? When you find yourself alone with only yourself and the Spirit? Left to experience your very own thoughts and your very own beliefs? What happens in the quiet of the night, when you find yourself, all alone, in your own thoughts? What do those moments feel like to you? Are they lonely? Are they frightening? Or, rather, are they truly satisfying? At the end of it all, this is the significance and the importance of belief and of thought. Your life is entirely your very own, and it is the direct result of what you believe – of what you continue to think. And so, how is your faith contributing to that life? How are your beliefs helping to bring about everything that you've been promised? Is your faith, as genuine and as sincere as it is, serving to propel you into a life of greater abundance, or is it causing you to retreat backward, into greater fear, greater paranoia, and even more lack? Only you can answer that for yourself, within your very own life.

What is it like to be left within your very own mind? You see, my friend, the issue truly isn't GOD, the issue isn't your adversary, and it really isn't even the struggles you face. The issue is what you *believe* about your struggles and, furthermore, what you believe about your very own self. Numerous times throughout the passages of the Holy Bible, the scriptures make mention of the very real and very important principle of repentance. Countless times, in fact, the scriptures demand that we "repent." From the Word of the Lord through the prophets of old to the nation of Israel while in Babylonian captivity, to John the Baptist, the great forerunner of the gospel crying in the wilderness, to Jesus himself saying that repentance and the remission of sins would be preached beginning at Jerusalem, and to the early apostles who ushered in a very literal age of the miraculous, the theme of repentance is replete throughout the entirety of the sacred texts. The act of repentance, though, means something vastly different than what most of us have for so long been led to believe. Once again, it seems, theatrics and showmanship have contributed to both the preaching and the understanding of this sacred, solemn responsibility. Repentance means, quite simply, to change one's mind and to shift one's focus – simply to turn away from the old beliefs and old paradigms and to turn toward a newness of life and a new way of thinking.

Not only is repentance necessary for all; as the scriptures continuously remind us, there is no new life without it. In order to begin to experience the greater and the more abundant life within the Kingdom which Jesus preached, we must have a change of mind. We must shift our focus toward the more heavenly, more spiritual things and away from the lower, more darkened elements of existence. Repentance, though, contrary to the popular teaching of religion, is not simply a singular, one-time occurrence that takes place at the altar of a beautiful, ornate sanctuary. No. Instead, repentance is a daily occurrence. When thoughts of negativity come, change your mind. When you begin to see yourself as defeated and as less-than, change your mind. When you begin to feel that struggle is just some necessary evil that must be endured in this world, change your mind. And, above all, when you begin to see yourself as separate from GOD and as nothing more than a depraved, fallen soul undeserving of and unworthy of the abundant life you've been promised, by all means, change your mind! This simple act of shifting focus is the Biblical meaning of repentance. As you can see, once you begin to move away from the theatrics and the showmanship surrounding popular teachings, what you will find is something real, something genuine, and, most importantly, something that possesses the power to truly sustain.

In his second epistle to the newly established church at Corinth, the Apostle Paul speaks emphatically about the importance of repentance and shifting focus by writing of the importance of *"Casting down imaginations, and every high thing that exalteth itself against the knowledge of God, and bringing into captivity every thought to the obedience of Christ." (2 Corinthians 10:5 KJV)* As you can see, repentance and a shifting of perspective is essential to the experiencing of an abundant life, and the true shift takes place within the mind – within what Paul refers to the "imaginations." An imagination, as you've seen, though, is simply an inner "image" which you've chosen to give place to and to focus upon. Did you know that your life – the life that you now find yourself living and experiencing on a daily basis – is simply the outward, external "image" of an internal "image" that you've given place to? It's true. Everything stems from within our own selves, from within our own minds and hearts, as the scriptures repeatedly bear out to us. And so, my friend, if you now find yourself unsatisfied and discontented with the imagery around you then it's time you finally, once and for all, get serious about changing the imagery within your very own thoughts!

Right now, if you find yourself living a life of constant struggle and constant attack, then you've at some point in your life exalted all of your incorrect thoughts – thoughts that are contrary to the truth of Christ. Did you know that you possess the divine, sovereign, and innate power of discernment, even when you aren't fully activating it? You possess the power to discern and to analyze each and every passing thought that enters into your mind, choosing in each moment whether to focus upon it or to neglect it. The scriptures make mention of this divine gift of discernment in this way: *"For the word of God is quick, and powerful, and sharper than any twoedged sword, piercing even to the dividing asunder of soul and spirit, and of the joints and marrow, and is a discerner*

of the thoughts and intents of the heart."
(Hebrews 4:12 KJV) This passage of scripture recorded from the writer of Hebrews gives us what is, perhaps, the single, greatest revelation concerning our thoughts and the power of our beliefs: that our beliefs possess *intentions*.

We so often speak of "intention" in such a flippant and trivial way, as if intentions possess very little meaning. You've heard it defined, I'm sure, as nothing more than a "choice." "That wasn't my intention," some say. Or, "I don't intend to do that." Or, better yet, "I was intending to take the trash out, but I forgot." Intention is often depicted as nothing more than random occurrence – so very vague and so inconsequential. The truth of the matter, though, as the writer of Hebrews reminds us, is that absolutely nothing is ever really unintentional. If you said something in a harsh way, it wasn't unintentional; it was a conscious choice. It you didn't take out the trash, it wasn't unintentional; you simply chose not to. And, furthermore, if you are living a life of struggle and constant warfare, it isn't unintentional; you're facing it because it's the intention you continue to set for your life based upon your focus! My friend it's time to begin to repent – to turn away from old, limiting beliefs that are no longer serving you. It's time to have a shift of perspective and a change of focus. It's time to begin to develop a new, inner "image" by which to build your life and the world around you. It's time to tear down the "images" – the "idols" that you've erected on the "high places" of your mind.

THE GOODNESS

"Goodness is the only weapon you need."

If you've followed my work or my writings for any length of time, then you know I'm a firm believer that energy is its own self-fulfilling prophecy. Meaning, quite simply, that the energy we give place to within or thoughts will continue to manifest and will continue to expand. Energy, in and of itself, in its pure form is always neutral. It possess only the intention that we place into it. And just as the energy of goodness continues to grow and to flourish when it is focused upon and meditated upon and pondered, the energy of negativity does the same. The life you now find yourself living is the direct result of the energy you've given place to and the direct result of your own intentions, based entirely upon your thoughts and your very own beliefs about yourself and the world around you. Your adversary would love nothing more than to cause you to become forgetful or neglectful of your own unlimited and creative power. You possess the very nature of the Godhead, bodily, just as Jesus. The first epistle of John, in fact, reminds of us this. *"Herein is our love made perfect, that we may have boldness in the Day of Judgment: because as he is, so are we in this world." (1 John 4:17 KJV)*

Now, think of your own days of judgment – those days when you've judged yourself far too harshly and forgotten your promises of an abundant life. Think of those many, many countless times in which you've judged every obstacle and every moment of hardship as nothing more than an attack of the devil, set on destroying you or ruining your life. Think of the judgements that, as a result, you've inadvertently placed upon those around you because you've judged yourself and have judged your own life. In those moments, you've become forgetful and neglectful of your true identity. The truth, though, in spite of what it may feel like, is that you are the Creator. As He is, so are we. The scriptures could not be any clearer in the matter regarding our true identity. The very nature of the Creator is the nature that we possess, and, as a result, you and I are daily creating the lives that we experience. We are constantly, ceaselessly crafting the world around us based entirely upon our very own thoughts.

And now, think of the all the good. In spite of all the moments of struggle, all the moments of hardship, and all the many, many moments of life which can feel so very draining, at times, you and I have so, so very much to be thankful for. We have so much goodness all around us in this vast, great and beautiful world. In case you haven't realized it yet, the world – your world – will continue to exist in the way that you choose to see it. According to some, the world is getting darker and darker, as evil continues to abound and as all hope seems to increasingly diminish. That's not my world, though. That's not the world I enjoy. According to some, the world will only get worse and worse, more blackened and stained with sin and with debauchery until the judgment of the LORD brings utter and complete annihilation. That's not my world, though. Whenever I hear such claims, I have to admit, I often find myself wondering just exactly what world they're referring to. Again, I say, that's not *my* world. That's not the world I live in and experience each day.

No, instead, *my* world is a world fill with more blessing than I can even comprehend. *My* world is filled with beauty and abundance and total and complete prosperity. In my world –

the world that I experience daily – I find myself overtaken with abundance. My world is the Kingdom coming to earth, just as Jesus prayed. Allow me to, for a moment, give you a glimpse into *my* world. In my world, I awaken each day to enjoy a life that's filled with many wonderful and amazing people. I'm so blessed I can hardly find the words. I have so many wonderful and unique relationships. I have a beautiful family that I adore. I have wonderful friends who adore me. My life is filled with so many wonderful relationships of all sorts. I'm so blessed and so privileged to have a worldwide, global ministry that allows me to each day live out my passion and my love for all people throughout the world. I write books, sharing principles that I'm passionate about. Some have even become international bestsellers. I don't have to do that, though. I do that because I want others to know just how beautiful and how abundant like in the Kingdom can be. I don't have lack. I stopped believing in that years ago. I have a home that is the home of my dreams, and I live in prosperity. In the world that I live in, each and every day, I see good things, and I'm filled with the knowledge and goodness of a good and loving GOD.

Of course, it wasn't always this way, though. Years ago, I fought spiritual warfare too, just like you. Years ago, just like you, I was taught to view life as a constant, never ending struggle, filled with constant battles and a barrage of attack. Years ago, like you, I was taught to spend much of my day "binding" the enemy, rebuking the devil and preaching against everything that I didn't want. I didn't have an abundant life, though. Those things never once led me to feel satisfied or fulfilled. I never saw the good. And, as a result, I rarely, if ever, experienced it. So, thankfully, I changed my mind. What about you, though? What is your world like? What type of world do you live in and enjoy each day? The world that you awaken to each day – the life that you get to experience – what is *your* world like? How do you see it? How do you define it? The world, you see – the daily sphere of influence that we experience – is nothing but a result of our own definition. By divine and by a wonderfully intelligent design, as Creators, you and I are given the divine and heavenly ability to define our world. It was like this in the very beginning, also, when we were first given dominion. Somewhere along the way, religion began to make us feel that we had somehow, somewhere lost that ability. For me, though, I stopped believing that lie long, long ago. And today, I am so blessed to be able to experience the fruits of a rich and abundant life.

You see, my friend, something truly wonderful and remarkable begins to happen the moment that we choose to begin to focus upon the goodness. When we do, all of the sudden, spiritual warfare begins to seem so very, well, pointless and unnecessary. The battles and the fight just seem to become such an unnecessary waste of time and an unnecessary burden. It all starts to feel so overwhelming and so exhausting. It becomes so noticeably shallow and, well, downright childish. Life begins to change and so, too, does the world around us the moment we begin to realize that there are truly no wars left to fight and that the battlefield has always been and will continue to be within our very own minds. What if you could begin to see the goodness of the abundant life existing all around you, instead of seeing lack, hardship, and apparent chaos? The moment that you begin to change the way in which you see your world will be the beginning your world will change. We walk by faith and not by sight. This is not some magical premise of positive thinking; rather, it is a very real and very dynamic principle within the Kingdom.

(As it is written, I have made thee a father of many nations,) before him whom he believed, even God, who quickeneth the dead, and calleth those things which be not as though they were." *(Romans 4:17 KJV)* There are old dreams, old visions, and old promises – things that may seem dead to you – simply waiting to be recognized all over again. It's time to reactivate the abundant life that you've allowed to diminish and bring it to life once again! You do this, quite simply, by choosing to see it and making the choice to set your focus upon it. You will experience the world the way in which you choose to view it. I say this not to in any way make lite of very real moments of hardship, very real pains, and the very real ills of the world that we all experience at times. Jesus, himself, even reminded us that in this world there will always be moments of hardships and very real times of tribulation. These moments, though, are not lasting and never, ever have they

been intended to define the totality of life. Tribulation will come and go, but the goodness of the abundant life will exist forever. That is, if you make the choice to see the good.

Every good thing comes from GOD. *"Every good gift and every perfect gift is from above, and cometh down from the Father of lights, with whom is no variableness, neither shadow of turning." (James 1:17 KJV)* There is so much good, just waiting to be experienced and enjoyed, if only you would see it. Why dwell on the hardships and the moments of pain when, instead, you can begin to recreate your life and, in turn, recreate your own world by choosing your thoughts much differently than you have been? The powerful, heavenly Kingdom Law of Attraction is based entirely upon the command given in the very beginning to be fruitful and to multiply and to have dominion. This world – *your* world – is waiting to be experienced, enjoyed, and lived. For far, far, too long you've spend your energy fighting, warring against, and rebuking rather than living in, enjoying, fully experiencing and subduing! It's time for that to change. Stop fighting ceaseless and never ending religious wars to which there are no end in sight and begin, instead, to enjoy the life of your dreams.

Throughout years of prophetic counseling and empowerment coaching, I've had the tremendous privilege and the great honor of connecting with countless thousands of individuals, just like you, who have, as we all do, experienced the many pains of life. Pain, though, like all things, is simply a matter of perspective. Even in the greatest pain, there exists love and the ability to grow. Not so long ago, I had the honor of meeting Mandy, a single mother whose husband had recently passed. As we all feel during times of great pain, there were questions, there was anger, and there was a very real and overwhelming sense of loss. What I've realized, though, throughout my own journey is that our questions are alright. I assure you, my friend, GOD is strong enough to handle our uncertain moments, and it's alright to ask questions – even when the answers may not always seem very obvious. When Mandy reached out to me to inquire of the Word of the LORD, understandably, she was feeling overwhelmed by the darkness which seemed to surround her. When I first met Mandy, her husband, Michael, had passed only four short months prior after a long and debilitating struggle with cancer. There had been countless prayers offered. There had been intercession. There had been countless hours spent in travailing prayer. There had been months spent rebuking the sickness and disease. In the end, though, Michael experienced his healing personally, when he returned home to Heaven. Although that wasn't the outcome that Mandy wanted, of course, Michael had found his healing and is now alive and well for all eternity.

When we face moments of pain so very real and so very overwhelming that that they shake us to our very core, often times, there are no real answers which can satisfy our questions. In these moments, it is faith which must be relied upon as never before. For Mandy, I couldn't explain to her why Michael had gone home to be with the LORD. I couldn't provide her with the answers to questions about how she should move forward. What can one possibly say to a single mother, left to raise an infant daughter after her husband has passed? To say that everything happens for a reason or that, simply, God knows best, although true, is nothing more than a cliché in the moment of pain and suffering. Within Christianity we seem to always know the right things to say, sometimes forgetting that our cheap, programmed, canned responses are nothing more than cheap platitudes. Mandy and I simply had a conversation, and in that conversation the presence of the LORD was with us. I could feel Him so very close to us in her moment of pain. To many, in those painful, dark months following Michael's passing, it seemed the enemy had been victorious. The spiritual warfare, it seemed, hadn't worked. The prayers had all gone unanswered. The months spend in travail didn't work. To Mandy, it seemed, she had lost her battle and the adversary had won. It simply wasn't true though.

You see, Michael, today, is just as alive as he'd ever been – even more alive, in fact. The cancer didn't take his life. Nothing can take our lives. For Michael, the cancer was simply the means by which he transitioned to return home to Heaven. The "enemy" had no say in the matter. In fact, imagine the surprise of the adversary when Michael returned home to Heaven, fully healed, fully whole, with no need to ever fight another battle again? Miracles happen when you begin to change your perspective, my friend. As Mandy and I spent time together, in conversation, something truly marvelous began to happen. The darkness began to dissolve and, before my very eyes, I watched as goodness began to envelop her. Suddenly, the questions ceased. She found herself thinking of her dear husband and of their love affair. Suddenly, her eyes began to light up with joy and with nostalgia. She told me about how the two of them had met while attending the same university. Michael was ever the practical joker. When he first asked Mandy out on a date, being the practical joker that he is, he simply handed her a hand-written note. It read: "Will you go out with me? Check 'yes' or 'no.'" As she recounted to me wonderful, heartfelt, often hilarious stories from their time together, Mandy began to laugh hysterically. She was remembering the goodness of it all.

Now, each and every time Mandy looks to the face of her son, she sees Michael. He even has his personality. For Mandy, the many, many questions, although real, have seemed to become less significant – much less burdensome. Mandy is strong today and once again enjoying life because, rather than giving credit to some adversary, she chose to remember the goodness. She inspired me. And so, today, for you, I feel compelled to share with you a very simply strategy that will always, without fail, end the attack of the enemy every time. When the onslaught comes, remember the goodness. Rather than choosing to give credit to the pain, instead begin to give thanks for the many, many blessings existing within your life. I promise you that as you do, suddenly, spiritual warfare will become the last thing on your mind as you begin to realize just how much you truly have to give thanks for. Rather than choosing to give place to the darkness, give thanks instead.

When you do, you will begin to activate the heavenly power of Creation within your life and you will, in turn, begin to attract even more of the good. Everything around you exists exactly the way you choose to see it. Yes, moments of pain are very real. But so is goodness.

OUTER DARKNESS

"Sin is a life not fully lived in abundance."

The religious mind is angered whenever one begins to dismantle unbiblical spiritual warfare. I find myself often in a state of bewilderment when many sincere believers write to me or approach me after conferences and ask how I could have the audacity to speak against spiritual warfare or the enemy. Many ask, "Are you suggesting that there is no enemy, no devil, and no Hell?" Puzzled, I respond that although such things are indeed very real, they are simply undeserving of our time and attention. Why is it that the mindset of religion fights so ferociously to defend and to cling to ideas regarding darkness and the demonic? Though humanity is becoming ever-increasingly more open to greater revelations concerning the Kingdom of Heaven, where teachings regarding darkness and warfare are concerned, religion seeks to hold firm, unwavering in its desire to continue to cling to erroneous beliefs based in superstition and primitive, archaic ideologies. And so, yes, the darkness is a very real reality. However, contrary to the imaginative, conjured imagery that religion has for centuries sought to propagate, the reality of "Hell," "sin," and the demonic in no way resembles what most have been led to believe. Who is our adversary? Who are we warring against? And what of the accounts of demonic possession within the scriptures? If spiritual warfare is, in fact, based upon an unbiblical, erroneous false premise, what are we to do with the passages of scriptures regarding "demons," "Hell," and "outer darkness?"

The scared text of the Holy Scriptures is beautiful and awe-inspiring – given by the divine inspiration and transcribed by men as they were moved upon the Holy Spirit. Knowing that, though, to truly do justice to the text, a student of the sacred scriptures must also bear in mind the historical context, the religious context, and the cultural element of the audience of the time to whom the scriptures were first given. Many great injustices have been done and justified with unfounded, unwarranted interpretations of the text, all because we so often think that when the scriptures were transcribed, modern, American culture was within the minds of the writers. Nothing could be any more untrue. Though the scriptures serve as inspiration for the whole of humanity, contrary to popular belief, Jesus did not speak the English language, nor did his disciples. In order to understand the context of Biblical writings and to give proper exegesis to the text, one must understand that the scriptures are not American writings, or European writings, or

Asian writings; the scriptures are Jewish writings – emanating from Jewish culture. When the scriptures began to become transcribed, there was no "Christianity" as we know it today; it had yet to be fully established. As the disciples went about healing the sick and casting out "devils," there were no Bibles. There were no churches, as we now view them. There were no sermons regarding spiritual warfare. In fact, it would not be until well into the second and third century that core teachings which we refer to as "Christian" would even begin to become canonized. To understand the time and the culture and the language of the Bible, one must first understand fully that what we now refer to as "Christianity" began, simply, as a spiritual movement that, at the time, was only beginning to differentiate itself from the religious Judaism of the day.

The world to which Jesus ministered and taught concerning the Kingdom was well aware of the prophets and of the Levitical law which had been handed down to Moses atop Mount Sinai. The Law – the Torah – was the basis of the religion commonly practiced at the time. Pharisees and Sadducees and those of the Sanhedrin were scholars – not of the scriptures that we now refer to as the "Holy Bible" but of the Law which had been handed down to Moses. In the religion of the time in which Jesus walked, there was knowledge of the Law and of the prophets – and there was a great deal of mysticism and mythology that had been passed down through generations. Divination and magic and even sorcery were common place and practiced even by some religious Jews of the time, as evidenced within the Book of Acts, where we find one Simon the Sorcerer gaining a large following and even converting disciples of his own. I share this to say that as Jesus walked about teaching concerning the Kingdom of Heaven, the teaching seemed very mysterious and new and strange to the minds of those who first heard it, because for generations they had lived only with a belief in the Mosaic Law, legalistic practice, and deeply ingrained superstitions about darkness. This was the culture, though, to whom Jesus first began to minister, and this was the climate which would ultimately give rise to a movement which would, years later, come to be known as "Christianity." It was a very different time. And a very different world. Superstitious paranoia was so deeply ingrained, in fact, that many even feared traveling out after sundown, thinking that the darkness of the night symbolized a time in which the "underworld" had been given full reign until the following morning when the sun would rise again. Factor in, also, the beliefs that many Jews had adhered to while in Babylonian captivity and consider, also, the Greek mythology rampant in Roman places of worship in surrounding areas, and you find that the beliefs of the time were an amalgamation of many various primitive ideas, mythologies, and legalism.

And so, when Jesus spoke to the multitudes about topics such as "outer darkness" and "devils" and when he encountered the demoniac that we refer to as "Legion" and even when he healed the sick and performed miracles, he reached the multitudes where they were, using illustrations and stories – parables – that they could visualize and understand. As difficult as it might be to fathom such a different world, the fact is that in the culture of that time, talk of the "devil" was actually much more common and much more rampant than it even is today, if you can imagine that. Even the most basic of hardships was considered to be the work of "demons" or the result of some hidden "sins." So deeply ingrained within the consciousness of the time was the belief in "devils," really, that on numerous occasions even Jesus himself was accused of being under the control of demons. Yes, talk of demons was quite rampant. One notable example which serves to further confirm the superstitions of the time is the account recounted within the synoptic gospels in which Jesus healed the blind man. *"And as Jesus passed by, he saw a man which was blind from his birth. And his disciples asked him, saying, Master, who did sin, this man, or his parents, that he was born blind? Jesus answered, Neither hath this man sinned, nor his parents: but that the works of God should be made manifest in him. I must work the works of him that sent me, while it is day: the night cometh, when no man can work. As long as I am in the world, I am the light of the world. When he had thus spoken, he spat on the ground, and made clay of the spittle, and he anointed the eyes of the blind man with the clay, And said unto him, Go, wash in the pool of Siloam, (which is by interpretation, Sent.) He went his way therefore, and washed, and came seeing." (John 9: 1-7 KJV)*

This account gives what is perhaps the greatest insight into the common theology of the day and also gives a glimpse into even a mention of "night" and of "darkness." Notice, though, that when speaking of the darkness, Jesus is referring to the literal night sky, after sundown, and not of some malevolent underworld. Even the disciples who had already been in fellowship with Jesus for an extended period of time and had already been initiated in the teaching regarding the Kingdom believed that the man was blind as the result of some "sin" he had committed. They wondered even, if whether or not the blindness was the result of some generational curse, asking even if, perhaps, his parents were the ones who had originally sinned. The account within John chapter nine does not end simply with the miracle of healing, though. The account goes on and continues to give us even greater insight into the legalism and superstition which were so rampant in the beliefs of the time, as we are shown a sort of "inquisition," as the healed man is interrogated by religious leaders of the day. On numerous instances throughout his interrogation, as he's questioned regarding his healing, the issue of "sin" is repeatedly brought up continuously.

"The neighbours therefore, and they which before had seen him that he was blind, said, Is not this he that sat and begged? Some said, This is he: others said, He is like him: but he said, I am he. Therefore said they unto him, How were thine eyes opened? He answered and said, A man that is called Jesus made clay, and anointed mine eyes, and said unto me, Go to the pool of Siloam, and wash: and I went and washed, and I received sight. Then said they unto him, Where is he? He said, I know not. They brought to the Pharisees him that

aforetime was blind. And it was the sabbath day when Jesus made the clay, and opened his eyes. Then again the Pharisees also asked him how he had received his sight. He said unto them, He put clay upon mine eyes, and I washed, and do see. Therefore said some of the Pharisees, This man is not of God, because he keepeth not the sabbath day. Others said, How can a man that is a sinner do such miracles? And there was a division among them. They say unto the blind man again, What sayest thou of him, that he hath opened thine eyes? He said, He is a prophet. But the Jews did not believe concerning him, that he had been blind, and received his sight, until they called the parents of him that had received his sight. And they asked them, saying, Is this your son, who ye say was born blind? how then doth he now see? His parents answered them and said, We know that this is our son, and that he was born blind: But by what means he now seeth, we know not; or who hath opened his eyes, we know not: he is of age; ask him: he shall speak for himself. These words spake his parents, because they feared the Jews: for the Jews had agreed already, that if any man did confess that he was Christ, he should be put out of the synagogue. Therefore said his parents, He is of age; ask him. Then again called they the man that was blind, and said unto him, Give God the praise: we know that this man is a sinner. He answered and said, Whether he be a sinner or no, I know not: one thing I know, that, whereas I was blind, now I see. Then said they to him again, What did he to thee? how opened he thine eyes? He answered them, I have told you already, and ye did not hear: wherefore would ye hear it again? will ye also be his disciples? Then they reviled him, and said, Thou art his disciple; but we are Moses' disciples. We know that God spake unto Moses: as for this fellow, we know not from whence he is. The man answered and said unto them, Why herein is a marvellous thing, that ye know not from whence he is, and yet he hath opened mine eyes. Now we know that God heareth not sinners: but if any man be a worshipper of God, and doeth his will, him he heareth. Since the world began was it not heard that any man opened the eyes of one that was born blind. If this man were not of God, he could do nothing. They answered and said unto him, Thou wast altogether born in sins, and dost thou teach us? And they cast him out." (John 9:8-34 KJV)

And so, throughout the account within John chapter nine, we find that not only did Jesus' own disciples believe that sin was the cause of the blindness but that such a belief was common throughout the entire region. This account serves as confirmation of the theology which ran rampant throughout the day. Notice that, here, again, a reference is made accusing even Jesus himself as being the "adversary" and performing miracles by other means. And, then, even after the parents of the healed man were interrogated, no answers sufficed. Even in the end, the man who had just received his miraculous healing was cast out of the temple and labeled a "sinner," in part for having been blind to begin with and, in part, for having been healed of his blindness. As you can see, it's impossible to win with religion. You can't debate it. You can't answer it logically. You can't reason with it. You must oppose it. Jesus new this better than all others, which is why when he was speaking to the multitudes concerning the Kingdom of Heaven, he continuously used imagery and language they would understand. When ministering and teaching, he used the language of the day, addressing principles and beliefs that were common to the time and common to the region. To reach the intended audience, Jesus continually relied upon the imagery of the day.

When speaking of being "cut off" and cast into "outer darkness," he was referencing Levitical Law which forbade work at night time and was also playing upon the imagery of the superstition of darkness to illustrate the power of the "light" and of "illumination."

The term "devil" is derived from the Hebrew term "sair," which simply means "goat" and was used in reference to the carved, graven images of woodland or forest creatures commonly worshipped by the heathen. The term "demon," originating from the Hebrew term "shed," meaning "idol," is depicted within Greek in the New Testament accounts of demonic possession as "daimon," quite literally referring to anything that is allowed to "control." Throughout the centuries, though, through various traditions having been passed down and through various mythologies of Roman times, what began as merely terms used to refer to anything and everything that is focused upon and given control became personified to literal entities, beings, and figures of darkness. The term "satan," in fact, quite literally means "one who opposes." Knowing this, I find it of interesting note that Jesus one referred to Peter as "satan" when Peter objected to the crucifixion. And so, as you can see, yes, "demons," "devils," "satan," and even the "outer darkness" are very real indeed. However, they're not what religion has led you to believe. For centuries, religion has erroneously propagated lies steeped in myth, superstition, and, truly, a great deal of exaggeration. In truth, the "demonic," based upon the true linguistics of the original text, refers to the "images," the "idols" and the "imaginations" that we allow to "control" us, which keep us from living an abundant life. There really isn't need to place more personification into such things and to exaggerate them beyond their importance. Though topics such as Hell, the demonic, and even sin are, in fact, very real and much warranted topics of discussion; the truth of the matter is that now, today, the modern culture that we now find ourselves within views these topics based upon an entirely false premise – a lie. Yes, these things are real; however, they are not what you've been led to believe. There are images and imaginations that for so long you have allowed to influence your thinking and your faith, images that have kept you from living out an abundant life and from prospering to your fullest potential within the Kingdom.

As the blind man was healed, notice, again, the response of Jesus when questioned about "sin" and its effects. When asked if the blindness had been caused by the man's sin or by the sins of his parents, Jesus responded, quite simply, "Neither." In other words, to put it another way, moments of hardship have nothing to do with an "enemy." Literally everything exists so that the works of GOD might be made manifested within the earth. I find myself often thinking of just how shocking and how very strange the teaching of the inner Kingdom must have seemed to those who first heard it all those years ago. Imagine the bewilderment of the religious, as they heard Jesus speak. It must have seemed like utter and complete blasphemy. To say that Heaven existed within all men and woman and that the enemy had no role to play in the matter must have seemed like absolute heresy. The truth which Jesus shared ultimately led to his torture and execution. However, today, even now, the gospel is continuing to be proclaimed throughout the earth as, day by day, moment by moment, men and women are becoming awakened to the greater truths of the inner Kingdom of Heaven, becoming inspired to move away from superstitious beliefs and primitive, limited thinking, to experience a truly abundant and truly prosperous life.

FORGETTING THE MONSTERS

"The Gospel has always been about human beings."

Each day, in each moment, the Gospel is going forth throughout the world, and each moment a soul becomes awakened to the revelation of an abundant and rich life, Christ returns again. Yet, when we succumb to the myths and to the fables of religion, we disconnect ourselves from our own ability to live out an abundant and rich life. The term "gospel," quite literally meaning good news, has for decades been the driving force behind the global ministry and outreach of Identity Network. For years, I have been so incredibly privileged and fortunate to have witnessed countless thousands of lives transformed by the good news, and I've watched as, often before my very eyes, souls became awakened to the truth of Christ. There is nothing that has transformative power like the Gospel – the good news that having become awakened to Christ in us we are free to live out an abundant and a rich life. If you now find yourself living out a life within your own, daily existence, which seems so draining, so hopeless, and so filled with constant, daily attack and hardship, my heartfelt and sincere prayer is that by now you have begun to see that the hardship stems from your very own unbiblical, unfounded beliefs and the lies of man-made religions. Never were you destined to live a life of constant war, constant lack, and ceaseless, never ending fighting. Religion told you that. And you believed it.

There is nothing that steals lives away quite like the erroneous and demonic lies about spiritual warfare. Throughout the centuries, countless billions upon billions of people, throughout every generation, have failed to experience the rich and abundant life promised them, as they were led to believe that they were unworthy and undeserving of such a life. By now, though, I hope that you have begun to become awakened within by the Holy Spirit to the truth that you are a divine and sovereign Creator within this earth realm, having been infused with the very nature of the Godhead. Is it not written, in fact, that we are all "gods?" When the fullness of time had come, Jesus came into the world and began to teach concerning the Kingdom of Heaven, reminding humanity of its true identity and its true birthright. He proclaimed the good news that, regardless of the past, everyone has access to an abundant and rich life because the Kingdom of Heaven exists *within.* It must have seemed so very radical and even blasphemous to the religious of the day. Even now, it still does, as the effects of religion's poison continues to flow through the hearts and minds of beautiful and sincere people, blinding them to the truth of their birthright and enabling them to set up vain "images" and imaginations within themselves. Nothing kills and steals quite like the lies of religion. Limiting belief is truly the greatest adversary we face. The "thief" and the "adversary," in fact," are not demons and devils; they are the lies we tell ourselves.

To better understand this, we are given the words of Jesus himself, in the synoptic gospel of John. *"Verily, verily, I say unto you, He that entereth not by the door into the sheepfold, but climbeth up some other way, the same is a thief and a robber. But he that entereth in by the door is the shepherd of the sheep. To him the porter openeth; and the sheep hear his voice: and he calleth his own sheep by name, and leadeth them out. And when he putteth forth his own sheep, he goeth before them, and the sheep follow him: for they know his voice. And a stranger will they not follow, but will flee from him: for they know not the voice of strangers. This parable spake Jesus unto them: but they understood not what things they were which he spake unto them. Then said Jesus unto them again, Verily, verily, I say unto you, I am the door of the sheep. All that ever came before me are thieves and robbers: but the sheep did not hear them. I am the door: by me if any man enter in, he shall be saved, and shall go in and out, and find pasture. The thief cometh not, but for to steal, and to kill, and to destroy: I am come that they might have life, and that they might have it more abundantly. I am the good shepherd: the good shepherd giveth his life for the sheep. But he that is an hireling, and not the shepherd, whose own the sheep are not, seeth the wolf coming, and leaveth the sheep, and fleeth: and the wolf catcheth them, and scattereth the sheep. The hireling fleeth, because he is an hireling, and careth not for the sheep. I am the good shepherd, and know my sheep, and am known of mine. As the Father knoweth me, even so know I the Father: and I lay down my life for the sheep. And other sheep I have, which are not of this fold: them also I must bring, and they shall hear my voice; and there shall be one fold, and one shepherd. Therefore doth my Father love me, because I lay down my life, that I might take it again. No man taketh it from me, but I lay it down of myself. I have power to lay it down, and I have power to take it again. This commandment have I received of my Father." (John 10: 1-18 KJV)*

In the above account, Jesus emphatically makes a declaration regarding the purpose of the Gospel, saying that the purpose of his very message is to cause men and women to experience an even greater, more abundant and rich life. However, notice, if you will, just how Jesus makes this declaration. He does so by pointing out a very real contrast. He says that there are "thieves" and there are "robbers" and that there are many others who will attempt to have an abundant life by alternate means. He refers to these "thieves" and "robbers" as "hirelings." And all throughout the passage, imagery is used to depict the importance of caring for "the sheep." And so, as we examine the text much more closely, we see that Jesus is saying there are many who attempt to do the work of the "shepherd," whose hearts are in no way truly concerned with the wellbeing of the sheep. What does it all mean? At first, even those who listened on had difficulty understanding what seemed to be such a cryptic teaching. In reality, though, Jesus himself explains the true meaning by elaborating, yet again, by making a very real, very poignant contrast – pointing to those who truly care for the sheep because they love the sheep and those who pretend to care for the sheep because they've been "hired" to do so. These "hirelings," according to Jesus, are the true enemy and the true "thieves" and "robbers." I promise you, my friend, that if you will allow this teaching to penetrate your mind, never again will you struggle fighting pointless, endless wars. Never again will you ever believe in the need to battle in spiritual warfare!

For decades, the church has erroneously and falsely taught that the "thief" and the "robber" are the "devil," his "demons," and the malevolent forces of darkness. Notice, though, that nowhere in the entire passage does Jesus speak of otherworldly forces or even hint at the existence of such things! He doesn't refer to what the "devil" does; he refers to what people do! He isn't referring to demons; he's referring to people! Oh, my friend, I pray that you will receive this truth and become awakened in the Holy Spirit as never before. For centuries there have been PEOPLE – not demons – who have worked as "hirelings," claiming to care for the sheep but never once truly having best interest of the sheep in mind! Does this sound familiar to you? Jesus refers to the actions of those people – those placed with guarding and caring for the sheep – as theft and as robbery! This is without a doubt the single greatest passage depicting the evil and the dangers of religious false teachings. The thief and the robber aren't the devil or some demon, my friend. The thief and the robber are the religious lies you've been told and led to believe! Believing those lies is what has robbed you of an abundant life and kept you feeling trapped within a never ending, religious war with no end in sight. The lies that you have been led to believe have always been your ONLY adversary in this life. The "adversary," in fact, is the false and limiting belief you've been basing your life upon.

Even the most sincere, the most genuine, and the most heartfelt belief can be deadly and damning if it is untrue. Even the most genuine, passionate, and fervent faith does not equal truth if the faith is built upon a false premise. Perhaps you've heard the term "red herring" before? It's a term quite often used to depict an idea that is purposely intended and crafted to be misleading intentionally. Spiritual warfare and the religious beliefs that fuel it are the ultimate "red herring!" It's based upon a false premise and a faulty foundation having no basis in reality. My friend, like the illusion of a magician, it's all smoke and mirrors and nothing more. Yet, through the power of orthodoxy, under the guise of "spiritual authority," this lie had been labeled as unquestionable, undeniable truth, and you've been told to never dare even entertain the notion that your beliefs may very well be incorrect. To question your beliefs would be heresy, we're told. No "faithful" follower of Christ would ever dare to question their beliefs, right? But, yet, within the account depicted in the gospel of John chapter ten, we find the true "shepherd" – the shepherd, who has a heart for the sheep, knows the needs of the sheep and is concerned for their safety. My friend, do you truly believe that religion has ever had your best interest at heart? Has religion, ever, at any point truly wanted you to prosper? Or has it, rather, simply wanted you to "parrot" and to mimic its actions, its messages, and its vain philosophies in an attempt to recruit others? What I mean to ask, quite simply, is are your beliefs truly leading you toward a more abundant life and into a deeper, more experiential relationship with the Spirit, or are they demanding your loyalty, your money, your continued participation, and your allegiance to the cause of the unholy war known as "spiritual warfare?" When will it end? The choice is yours and yours alone.

Even the most palatial and most wondrous and exquisite of homes, when built upon an unstable foundation, crumble to ruin. To say it another way, just because it may look and seem beautiful doesn't mean it will last. One need only refer to the passage in which Jesus spoke of the wise and the foolish builders to better understand just how damaging false, unbiblical, limiting beliefs can be. *"Therefore whosoever heareth these sayings of mine, and doeth them, I will liken him unto a wise man, which built his house upon a rock: And the rain descended, and the floods came, and the winds blew, and beat upon that house; and it fell not: for it was founded upon a rock. And every one that heareth these sayings of mine, and doeth them not, shall be likened unto a foolish man, which built his house upon the sand: And the rain descended, and the floods came, and the winds blew, and beat upon that house; and it fell: and great was the fall of it."* (Matthew 7:24-27 KJV) Every revelation will be tested throughout the trials and the pains of life. And so I would ask you, my friend, when you need your faith the most, is that faith – that belief – truly leading you toward a more abundant, more fulfilling life? Or, is it, instead, leading you to feel the need to continuously struggle and live in lack, always warring against demons, devils, and darkness rather than stepping out into a life of promise and fulfillment? If the answer is the latter rather than the former, then someone has lied to you, and you've chosen to build your house upon that lie.

Your beliefs and your thoughts form the basis of your life. Everything you do, attempt to do, or ever even consider attempting to do stems from the underlying beliefs and thought that you have made the basis of your life experience. This is why, according to the universal and heavenly Law of Attraction, if you want to recreate your life and change your life, you must change your thoughts. This is why Provers 4:7 declares, *"Wisdom is the principal thing; therefore get wisdom: and with all thy getting get understanding."* As we build and craft our lives each day, based upon our thoughts, continuously building, line upon line and precept upon precept, it is imperative that we examine, reexamine, and always strive to analyze not only what it is that we believe but also why it is that we believe what we believe. By building upon a faulty foundation, quite literally everything will become unstable and subject to impending catastrophe. What you believe, right now, today, is the cause of literally everything that you're experiencing within your life. As sincere, as genuine, and well-intentioned as you have been, somewhere along the way, long, long ago, you allowed the lies of limited thinking to begin to cloud your judgement and affect your perspective of yourself, of GOD, and of the purpose and true meaning of your life. As a result, for far, far too long you've lived beneath your means, choosing to believe that you are the victim of endless, ceaseless wars in the heavens rather than a powerful, divine Creator, crafted in the very image and in the very likeness of GOD. This limited, faulty belief has not only provided you with an unstable foundation, but years of continuous limited, faulty belief have eroded away what little foundation once existed, as you now find yourself living a life of such uncertainty. Where there was once strong faith, now, there is confusion. Where there was once joy and overwhelming abundance, now there lack and constant struggle. Somewhere along the way, long, long ago, you were introduced to teachings which falsely accused you of being inferior, being depraved, and being a mere "sinner," having somehow fallen from grace. These lies of limiting belief are the true "accuser of the brethren." Fortunately, though, in a moment – in the twinkling of an eye – you can become changed, as you awaken to truth and are able to move toward greater glories. Just as you and I have been given the powerful divine ability to create, thankfully, we can also begin to recreate. In order recreate, we need only to shift our focus.

Your beliefs have become the principles by which you live and by which you act in all areas of your daily life. There's a reason, you see, why Proverbs declares that wisdom is the very "principle" thing. Wisdom is foundational. In Paul's epistle to the church at Ephesus, he reminds the church, of the literal truth regarding beliefs. *"For we wrestle not against flesh and blood, but against principalities, against powers, against the rulers of the darkness of this world, against spiritual wickedness in high places." (Ephesians 6:12 KJV)* Upon first glance, at first notice, we see something quite familiar. This passage of scripture, perhaps more than all others, has been used to promote a teaching which says our battle is not with people but with demons and malevolent, mysterious forces exiting in the ether, set upon our destruction. When you closely examine the passage, though, you begin to see that such is simply not the case. The Apostle Paul reminds the church in his writing that the true battle is against "principalities." The term is derived from the root word "principle." My friend, there's simply no need to exaggerate or to use hyperbole or to be carried away with unnecessary theatrics or fear. The issue is much simpler than you've been led to believe all these years. The issue, quite simply, is that you've built your life upon wrong "principles." In order to change and to recreate your life and your life experiences, you need only to adapt to different principles. Notice, though, that within the passage of the Pauline epistle, the apostle makes mention, once again, of the term "high places." Remember that these "high places" are used simply to denote idolatry and imagery. What Paul was, in fact, saying to the church at

Ephesus was that because they had adapted to incorrect principles and faulty teachings, they had, in turn, created "images" and vain "imaginations" within their minds based upon a faulty premise. If you want to recreate your life, you need to begin to reassess the "principles" that you were once taught to live by.

Day in and day out, moment by moment, you and I are constantly and continuously being given the opportunity to reassess, recalibrate, and, in turn, recreate our lives based upon what we believe. The truth of the matter is that as we grow and evolve within the Kingdom, continuously being changed and ushered from greater glory into greater glory, we are often asked to consider letting go of old paradigms of thinking. What may have well worked for you ten, twenty, or even thirty years ago – or even as recently as yesterday – no longer serves you. There are beliefs that simply stopped working and stopped benefitting you a long, long time ago. As you examine these certain beliefs more closely, though, what you begin to find is that many of these old beliefs never truly benefitted you or served you at all. You only thought they did. My friend, contrary to what religion has told us, it is possible to be genuine, while being genuinely wrong. Healing begins and freedom comes the moment – the very instant – we recognize that we truly possess the power to shape our lives and our destinies and to experience a rich, abundant life. Somewhere along the way, you were robbed. Today is the day to finally, once and for all, to reclaim the promise of your birthright within the Kingdom of Heaven. That promise is the promise of an abundant   life.

THE ART OF WAR

"Have an ear to hear what the Spirit is saying to you, about you."

It was Lao Tzu who famously wrote in *The Art of War*, "The enemy of my enemy is my friend." The writings of Lao Tzu have been used and implemented throughout history by the great military minds and strategists throughout the world to better understand their opponent, to gain greater insight into the battlefield, and to better recognize ways to advance against the adversary in literal, physical times of war here in the earthly realm. I felt inspired by the Holy Spirit as I began writing to you to include what I believe to be one of the most powerful and most inspiring lessons I've ever learned within my own life, throughout years of international, prophetic ministry. Throughout the pages of this book, you and I have journeyed together through the history and the philosophy and the theology of the sacred text of the scriptures in an effort to completely annihilate and to dismantle the false and erroneous teachings regarding spiritual warfare which have become so rampant throughout the Christian faith. My heartfelt prayer for you, your own life, your family, and for those who would come after you in future generations, is that you begin to awaken to the truth of the reality of Christ and refuse to settle for the lifeless and limited beliefs of man-made religions. Throughout the pages of this book, you and I, together, have delved deeply into the truth of the sacred text and have discovered that spiritual warfare, for years, has been merely the product of our very own crippling and debilitating fears, stemming from the paranoia of our own fear-based, religious mindsets.

Prayerfully, you now know who and what your enemy is not. But, for a moment, in closing, I'd like for you to consider just who your enemy truly is? Who is the real enemy? Who is the "adversary?" So much can so often become lost in translation, particularly where theological belief is concerned, as meaning and as definition is placed upon certain words and phrases. Would you believe that not even once within the entirety of the scriptures does the text ever once say that Satan is the "enemy" of GOD? I would challenge you to find even a singular verse or passage claiming that the enemy of GOD is the devil, or demons, or any dark and malevolent figure, or Satan. I assure you that such a verse or passage simply does not exist. You see, what most of humanity, particularly within the church, have failed to recognize is that "adversary" in no way means "enemy." The two terms are simply in no way synonymous. Furthermore, "opposition" in no way is synonymous with "attack." Sure, in trying moments it may often times *feel* like an attack; however we are not called to be led by feelings; we walk by faith, instead. What if you could learn to see that "opposition" doesn't mean "attack?" Would that not only change and completely revolutionize the way in which you view your "adversary" but also completely change the way in which you choose to view any and all of the trying and seemingly difficult moments you now find yourself facing? To better understand this principle of the Kingdom, we must reassess and reevaluate what we refer to as "opposition." In "adverse" moments of trial and hardship, is there a greater reason for it all? Is there a lesson to be learned, even in all of the seemingly adverse moments of life?"

To find the answer, let us, for a moment, return to the very beginning of it all, back to where it all began. There was a man. There was a woman. And there was the Spirit of all

Creation. As the Creator introduced his crowning achievement to what would be their new home, he reminded them that everything was "good" and that they possessed absolute dominion and sovereignty over it all. As the Creator had breathed into them the very Breath of Life – the *ruach* – He infused them with His very own power to create. The newly formed world and its new inhabitants existed in total and absolute Oneness. They were like Him in every way, possessing His very own unique, sovereign intention. Man was given the task of labeling and defining the new world. Whatever man called the new Creation, *that* was its name. But, then, in an act of rebellion and utter defiance, it all changed in a moment – or so we have been led to believe. Man, being in absolute union with the divine and existing in total and complete solidarity and Oneness, suddenly, in a moment of temptation, took on a mind of his own. Well, at least according to the religious account of Creation's story. And we are told that, as it all changed, a very literal, very cataclysmic "fall" transpired which was so devastating that the Creator suddenly found Himself forced to provide atonement for such an egregious and damnable sin. The sin was so overwhelmingly and shockingly egregious that the only atonement for such a horrible sin could come in the form of the Creator's very own Son, who would, generations later, be forced to give His own life as ransom in order that humanity could then be reconciled to GOD.

As man and woman tasted of the forbidden fruit, we are told that paradise ended. Chaos and disorder entered into the newly formed perfection, forcing the man and the woman from the garden to toil and to slave and to work – to struggle and to fight to survive. The struggle, we are told, was simply a necessary evil, forced to exist as recompense for the egregious sin committed. My friend, is it any wonder, really, why Apostle Paul admonished the early church to grow into maturity and to put away childish things? Paul says that when we are children, we act like children. We think like children. We speak of childish things. When maturity comes, though, we put away childish nonsense and put to rest once and for all the fairy tales of our youth. We are supposed to, at least. You see, my friend, the only fall that ever truly took place was within the mind of man. The fall never took place within the heart of the Creator. Even after having tasted of the so-called forbidden fruit, even then, the Creator came to walk with them in the cool of the day, just as He always had. What could have possibly driven a divine man and a divine woman to partake of the forbidden fruit to begin with? And it is here that we are first shown the "image" of the "adversary." In the very beginning, the "adversary" is shown as a cunning and crafty serpent, so manipulative and so very much the "enemy" of the Creator that he would stop at nothing to lead the newly formed man into sin and into disobedience, thereby thrusting all of Creation into oblivion and into generation upon generation of total darkness and depravity.

In order to better understand this "adversary," though, one would need to examine the wiles which he employed. What did he say? What presentation could possibly have even made that would cause a divine man and a divine woman – both "gods" – to so desire the taste of a specific fruit from a specific tree? The serpent had said to the woman that if the fruit would simply be but tasted, she and the man would suddenly become like GOD. What seems to be casually omitted or neglected from all of the countless sermons and teachings regarding this, though, is the fact that the man and the woman already *were* like GOD. So identical in nature to GOD, in fact, were the man and the woman that absolutely nothing could have made them any more divine or sovereign. Somewhere, you see, in the midst of all the cunning craftiness of the serpent, interlaced within it all was a certain element of truth. Somewhere, even in the midst of the "temptation" – even in the midst of the work of the "adversary" – the Spirit was attempting to give a revelation to the man and the woman concerning their true identity. What if, rather than viewing moments of opposition and adversity as an attack of the "enemy" you instead chose to begin viewing them as opportunities to gain greater revelation and greater understanding? What if even in the midst of even the most adverse of situations, you found yourself able to ask, "What is the Spirit speaking to me through this?" Would such a decision not completely dismantle the need for spiritual warfare and put to rest any fear?

To better understand the role of the "adversary," we need only to be reminded of the account within the scriptures concerning the trials of Job. Contrary to what we have for years been led to believe about the "adversary," the account of Job reminds us that "adversary" does not mean "enemy." Throughout the passage detailing the many pains, the many trials, and the many, many moments of adversity Job faced, rather than being shown the "adversary" as an "enemy" of GOD, we find him, instead, being depicted as an "agent" of GOD – an agent of testing, working in tandem with GOD to reveal a greater level of faith within the servant of the LORD. Oh, I promise you that if you could begin to see even your greatest moments of trial as moments of opportunity never again would you ever feel the need to war! Even in the midst of your greatest trials, the Spirit is speaking. Let he who has an ear to hear, hear what he Spirit is saying to the church! And what the Spirit is saying is that adversity is NOT attack! It is opportunity for growth and increasing revelation! What if the church truly believed that Christ is the head of all things, as it has consistently claimed for centuries? Can you imagine the immense power and the immense revelation that would be gained and harnessed if we would simply believe what the scriptures say that literally all things are being worked together for our good? We say that. You say that. You even peach that. But do you truly believe that?

"And we know that all things work together for good to them that love God, to them who are the called according to his purpose." (Romans 8:28 KJV) In Paul's epistle to the church at Rome, he offers a reminder that there is opportunity even in adverse moments of struggle and pain. For generations, we have so often heard countless messages preached and various lessons taught concerning this particular

passage of scripture. Usually, though, the messages are seemingly geared toward suggesting that even in "bad" moments "good" will eventually come in the end. I would humbly and respectfully submit to you, my friend, that in spite of what has happened, in spite of what the situations may have felt like, and in spite of what you were told to believe, the truth of the matter is that it was "good" the entire time. It's high time you craft a theology free from the contradictions of religion. Is not Christ the head of all things? Even the head of the church, as the epistles remind us? Are not all things by Him and for Him and through Him, existing for the purpose of his own good pleasure? If so then that can only mean that He possesses no enemy that is apart from Himself. In fact to even suggest that there is something else – someone else – apart from Him is to completely dismiss the very definition of sovereignty. The two beliefs cannot coexist –

the belief in a sovereign, omnipotent GOD and also the belief in an "enemy" of GOD. Part of reconciling your faith and making the decision to walk away once and for all from the unbiblical lies regarding spiritual warfare is the understanding that the "adversary" is not an "enemy" and that "opposition" isn't "attack."

The psalmist declared there is no place in existence separated from the Presence. *"Whither shall I go from thy spirit? or whither shall I flee from thy presence? If I ascend up into heaven, thou art there: if I make my bed in hell, behold, thou art there. If I take the wings of the morning, and dwell in the uttermost parts of the sea; Even there shall thy hand lead me, and thy right hand shall hold me. If I say, Surely the darkness shall cover me; even the night shall be light about me. Yea, the darkness hideth not from thee; but the night shineth as the day: the darkness and the light are both alike to thee."* (Psalm 139:7-12 KJV) Notice, within this passage we find an even greater truth and more transcendent reminder of the reality of the "adversary" – one which most never wish to acknowledge: "darkness" and "light" are one in the same. Because the Presence is so expansive, filling up the complete totality of all existence, there is no place in which the Glory does not exist. For this reason, there is no darkness. "Darkness," you see, is merely an illusion. The knowledge – the revelation and understanding – of the totality of the Presence will cause you to begin to understand that in each and every moment, even within the most seemingly "dark" of moments, there is light. *"For the earth shall be filled with the knowledge of the glory of the Lord, as the waters cover the sea." (Habakkuk 2:14 KJV)* Although the Glory of the LORD has filled all space, the words of the prophet remind us that the "knowledge" of this is required. In other words, my friend, it is time for you to begin to see and to know that the darkness is merely an illusion.

What if you truly believed what you claim to believe? Furthermore, what if the church would truly begin to believe what it has preached for centuries, that Christ is the head of *all* things? Can you begin to imagine a world in which even the moments of apparent darkness would begin to be viewed as merely lessons and as reminders of the Glory of GOD? What if you could begin to see that even in the seemingly "dark" and apparently most adverse of situations even then the Spirit of the LORD is present to reveal truth? No longer would you battle. No longer would you war. Most of all, my dear friend, no longer would you fear. Can you even imagine a world in which fear did not exist? That is a very real reality and is the end-result of a life having become truly awakened to the reality of the inner Kingdom of Christ which Jesus spoke of. For far too long, you've chosen, by your own choice, to live a life beneath your means, settling for less than what is truly yours. You have been deceived into neglecting your birthright, and, as a result, you have forgotten the true meaning of an abundant life. Rather than living without fear, you have become fearful, intimidated, condemned, and so insecure in your beliefs. You seem to have forgotten who you truly are.

In Paul's second epistle to the church at Corinth, he gives to the church a much needed reminder of the true battlefield – the mind and its thoughts. *"For the weapons of our warfare are not carnal, but mighty through God to the pulling down of strong holds;) Casting down imaginations, and every high thing that exalteth itself against the knowledge of God, and bringing into captivity every thought to the obedience of Christ." (2 Corinthians 10:4-5 KJV)* Rather than spending wasted days rebuking and casting out demons, begin to choose, instead, to cast down your own imaginations. The true battlefield, you see, has always been the mind. And the singular enemy has always come in the form of the incorrect thoughts we choose and allow ourselves to think. Today, as you read these words, you are being given a very real choice. You are being given the choice between blessing and cursing – a very real and stark contrast between life and death. Today, my sincere and most heartfelt prayer for you, for your family, and for them who would come after you is that you would choose life. Choose blessing, rather than cursing. You make this choice within your very own thoughts. For far too long you have allowed your imagination to run free. The time has come, though, to put away, once and for all, childish fables and begin to recognize the war is over. The war, for you, ends the very instant you   believe   it   has.

ABOUT THE AUTHOR

Dr. Jeremy Lopez is Founder and President of Identity Network and Now Is Your Moment. Identity Network is one of the world's leading prophetic resource sites, offering books, teachings, and courses to a global audience. For more than thirty years, Dr. Lopez has been considered a pioneering voice within the field of the prophetic arts and his proven strategies for success coaching are now being implemented by various training institutes and faith groups throughout the world. Dr. Lopez is the author of more than thirty books, including his best-selling books The Universe is at Your Command and Creating with Your Thoughts. Throughout his career, he has spoken prophetically into the lives of heads of business as well as heads of state. He has ministered to Governor Bob Riley of the State of Alabama, Prime Minister Benjamin Netanyahu, and Shimon Peres. Dr. Lopez continues to be a highly-sought conference teacher and host, speaking on the topics of human potential, spirituality, and self-empowerment. Each year, Identity Network receives more than one millions requests from individuals throughout the world seeking his prophetic counsel and insight.

ADDITIONAL WORKS

Prophetic Transformation

The Universe is at Your Command:
Vibrating the Creative Side of God

Creating With Your Thoughts

Crating Your Soul Map: Manifesting the
Future you with a Vision Board

Creating Your Soul Map: A Visionary
Workbook

Abandoned to Divine Destiny

The Law of Attraction: Universal Power of
Spirit

Prayer: Think Without Ceasing

And many, many more

Made in the USA
San Bernardino, CA
15 September 2019